ENDORSEMENTS

I recommend *Spent Matches* not because I consider Roy Moran a friend and mentor, but because in its pages we find the conviction to take honest inventory and the courage to ask ourselves and our churches, "If this really is God speaking, what are we willing to do about it, and who are we willing to tell?"

Allen Hoskyn
Methodist pastor, community chaplain, FCS Urban Ministries,
Lawrenceville, GA

Spent Matches is core, simple, easy to follow, and reproducible, anytime—anywhere. For the gospel to go viral and the Great Commission to be fulfilled will require all different kinds of churches, some just like this book talks about. Read it and apply it!

Bob Roberts Jr.
Author, *Bold as Love* and senior pastor, Northwood Church, Keller, TX

If there's anything that's needed among today's Christians, it's that we all go deeper and really follow through on Jesus' command to invest ourselves in other people and make disciples—even with our own children. In this book, Roy will give you a lot to think about in that regard, and will challenge you to live out your faith in ways that are more effective for the kingdom and more satisfying for us as well.

Carey Casey, CEO
National Center for Fathering

Roy is one of the few men who challenges and inspires me virtually every time we're together. *Spent Matches* captures what I have seen to be Roy's heart—a passion to creatively engage lost people with truth and turn them into communities of disciple-makers. This book will challenge you, trouble you, possibly irritate you, and ultimately inspire you. It is a thought-provoking wake-up call for the church to get back to doing what Jesus told us to do.

Dale Losch
President, Crossworld

If you are thin-skinned, don't read this book! But if you really want to look beyond our ego and natural self-protectionism to really understand where we are today as the American church, *Spent Matches* may be able to help you get there. After fully deflating any ego that might remain after reading the first section about where we are as a church today, Roy leads us through a thought-provoking process that challenges some of our most basic assumptions (some cherished assumptions) about church and ministry. Fortunately, the book doesn't end there. Roy goes on to offer up reasons to hope for a better church in the future. This hope, he tells us, is rooted in a fresh understanding of the Great Commission's laser focus on making disciples rather than planting churches. As we make disciples who make disciples, more and more churches will emerge in a process of accelerating growth.

> Dave Hunt, DMin
> Vice President of Disciple-Making Movements in the Americas
> Cityteam International

Rarely have I read a book that answered my questions, moved me to tears, gave practical insights that I can use immediately in ministry, and reignited passion for the Kingdom of God. *Spent Matches* by Roy Moran has done all that.

As a missions administrator focused on Disciple-Making Movements in Latin America, I have been asked numerous times if the DMM strategy could bear fruit in the United States. The answer is clear, and the answer is yes. This book explains how. No one who is concerned with finishing the Great Commission should miss this book.

> David Parish
> President, World Missions and Evangelism, Inc.

Discovering a different future for the church will not come from doing harder, better, or faster than what we've done in the past. In these liminal times we've got to think differently and do differently. Breakthrough ideas often are birthed at the intersection of disparate and conflicting ideas. Roy Moran invites us into that space to help transform "what could be" to "what will be."

> Eric Swanson
> coauthor, *The Externally Focused Church* and *To Transform a City*

Every page of this book will challenge the way you typically think about "church" and will give you hope that authentic "disciple-making disciples" communities can really happen on the earth. The thing I like most about my friend, Pastor Roy Moran, is that he is an "on-the-ground-practitioner" of the principles outlined in this book. He is doing the hard tedious work of living out a new way of doing church and challenging all of us in the process. If you really care about the future of the church and the expansion of the Gospel *Spent Matches* is a must read . . . but beware: you will be infected with a disciple-making mentality!

>Pastor Gary Schmitz
>Executive Director Citywide Prayer Movement, Kansas City

Spent Matches is the kind of book that all followers of Jesus Christ must read. Above all, this book has the ability to make us look inside and see our weaknesses: the kind and the depth of our Christianity. It makes us to see that we have a large and important task as a church to reach those who are far away from Jesus. On the other hand, it challenges us to look outside the box, beyond ourselves, as well as to glimpse a much larger mission: *The Missio Dei*, which all those who claim to be followers of Jesus, true disciples, should engage, so that the earth will be filled with the knowledge of God, as the waters cover the sea.

>Gustavo A. Chofard
>SEPAL/ OC International Missionary

Sobering truths but critical insights. This book gives key principles, pointing a way forward for the church to make progress in its mission to make disciples of all nations.

>Kevin King
>President, NYC International Project

Spent Matches is an important "state of the church" message thoughtful leaders will want to read. I was sobered as I read the book but also drawn in by Roy's engaging conversational style. If you want your church to make a difference in the world, this is essential reading.

>Floyd McClung
>All Nations Cape Town

Roy Moran is one unorthodox pragmatic leader, for whom Christianity is a faith and a lifestyle, not a religion! In this same manner, comes *Spent Matches* to reflect the mind-set of the author and lay for us the mission of the church in this world that is changing every day. One of the strengths of this book is that Roy lived and implemented it way before he wrote about it. It's the "raw" view of the church as Jesus intended it to be! *Spent Matches* is a must read for all those who passionately want to see a movement of God, founded on the Word of God, intended to love and obey God!

Nadim Costa
Executive Director, Near East Organization, Lebanon, and member of the City Council of Beirut

This book is a valuable guide and introduction to how North American followers of Jesus can be culturally relevant, biblically faithful, and fulfilled in Christ. Many folks feel that there must be another way to do church, but they don't know why they feel this way or where to begin. Roy has helped forge a path to how to remain culturally relevant to traditional notions of church gatherings in North America while also helping to unleash the rest of us to join the mission of God. No more holding back. No more telling people they aren't good enough or ready. In Jesus, all his promises are "Yes and Amen" for all of us messed up, theologically screwed up, sinner saints. If you are one of the "least of these," read to see how you can get started right here, right now, right where you are, and just as you are to partner with Jesus in his Great Commission.

Pam Arlund, PhD
Director of Training, All Nations Family – Kansas City Hub

Raw and real; provocative and practical. A brave and noble attempt to guide those on the cusp of total disengagement down a path of personal discovery and discipleship.

Pete Burney
Senior Executive, Corporate America

Roy Moran's book *Spent Matches* is an eye-opening book. It will help you to see the church in a bigger picture while looking through the lens of your understanding of kingdom vision and broadening your perspective of how we can win the world to Christ in a shorter period of time. In his book Roy expounds on the Great Commission found in Matthew 28. Roy explains clearly that the commission is for us to make disciples that make disciples. This concept is pure gold and is key to seeing closure to the Great Commission. This book builds beautifully on this principle and allows us to pick up a mirror and make an analysis of the heartfelt efforts that we have committed our lives to and sacrificed so much for. Sometimes the truth hurts us to the core, but only when we are hurting are we willing to change. I am thankful for the loving manner in which Roy wrote this book. It reaches into the heart of the matter while cautiously and carefully touching and challenging our hearts to change. Too many people are dying without Christ each day while we are allowing our methodologies and approaches to stand in the way of Christ's kingdom expansion. What will we do about it? Are we willing to change our methods and tactics so that we too will be able to see the Great Commission fulfilled in our lifetime? I recommend this book to all people who are passionate about finishing the task and are intensely awaiting the coming of our Lord and Savior Jesus Christ.

Randy Keith Travis Jr.
Third Generation Missionary and Co-Strategy Coordinator for the
Latin America DMM project with World Missions and Evangelism

Roy Moran is a trusted advisor to many, a chief agitator, uniquely skilled at bringing people "into close quarters with a revelation that creates discomfort in their paradigms" (see *From Teachers to Learning Designers*, chap. 4). His passion for pre-Christians and vision for a New Reformation is evident in these pages. If you are dissatisfied with the traditional approach to evangelism, you will find in *Spent Matches* a fresh approach worthy of consideration. If it causes discomfort, consider yourself blessed. A positive paradigm shift rarely takes place within the comfort zone.

Richard Potter
Musician and Writer, blogging at www.playingbyfear.com

This book from Roy Moran highlights the biblical concept of the Christian church as a "movement". . . not a "monument." He challenges the tendency of the church to focus on "maintenance" rather than on her "mission" as the body of Christ. He provides a solution by calling the church back to the great commission which refocuses her on obedience to Jesus' call to make disciples which will promote Church Planting Movements. After all it is "among the wolves that we are to find sheep." His experiences and passions have produced a helpful and practical challenge to the church of Jesus Christ. Shalom!

Rev. Victor John
Bhojpuri CPM Coach, Leadership Development

Roy Moran loves Jesus' church enough to tell us the brutal truth. Deep in our soul, we know that we as the church are failing the people of this world. In *Spent Matches*, Roy does not give simplistic answers, but rather digs beneath the surface of the necessary changes in belief and practice for us to live out Jesus' GREAT command: being disciples who make disciple-making disciples. Roy is not an arm-chair theologian but a local pastor who describes his journey with his fellow Shoal Creek disciples as they learn, struggle, fail, rejoice, and try again with lots of offbeat and refreshing efforts. Some would suggest that we abandon the existing church, but Roy shows us a hybrid path of how we as believers and churches can allow God to call us to a new Reformation of the church.

Stan Parks, PhD
DMM Trainer, VP Global Strategies, Beyond (beyond.org)

Spent Matches is not a light read. You may not want to keep it on your bedside table lest it disturb your sleep. The opening half reads like one of the Old Testament prophets. God's people are confronted by our unfaithfulness to his covenant. But like most of these prophecies, there is a way forward to avert the failures that appear sure. The audience most in need of trying this new option—a way between—is a traditional church that has been stirred into a state of wanting truly biblical disciple-making. What if you are daring enough to push through to the end? What if you will open your mind to a hybrid model of church? What if God can turn your nightmare into a new vision?

John Kenneth King
Director of Training and Strategic Access, Final Command Ministries

This is a book that every lay leader in churches across America should share with their entire church leadership team to challenge the paradigms of how they "do church."

J. D. Schlieman
Former Elder, Harvest Evangelical Church, Story City, Iowa

SPENT MATCHES

IGNITING THE SIGNAL FIRE FOR THE SPIRITUALLY DISSATISFIED

ROY MORAN

THOMAS NELSON
Since 1798

NASHVILLE   MEXICO CITY   RIO DE JANEIRO

Published in Nashville, Tennessee, by Thomas Nelson. Thomas Nelson is a registered trademark of HarperCollins Christian Publishing.

Thomas Nelson, Inc., titles may be purchased in bulk for educational, business, fund-raising, or sales promotional use. For information, please e-mail SpecialMarkets@ ThomasNelson.com.

Page design and layout: Crosslin Creative
Images: dollarphotoclub.com, vectorstock.com

Unless otherwise noted, Scripture quotations are taken from The Voice™ translation © 2012 Ecclesia Bible Society

Scripture marked KJV is from the King James Bible.

Scripture marked NET is from the NET Bible® copyright ©1996–2006 by Biblical Stud- ies Press, L.L.C. http://netbible.com All rights reserved.

The names: THE NET BIBLE®, NEW ENGLISH TRANSLATION COPYRIGHT © 1996 BY BIBLICAL STUDIES PRESS, L.L.C. NET Bible® IS A REGISTERED TRADE- MARK THE NET BIBLE® LOGO, SERVICE MARK COPYRIGHT © 1997 BY BIBLICAL STUDIES PRESS, L.L.C. ALL RIGHTS RESERVED

Scripture marked NIV is from HOLY BIBLE: NEW INTERNATIONAL VERSION®. © 1973, 1978, 1984 by International Bible Society. Used by permission of Zondervan Publishing House. All rights reserved.

Library of Congress Cataloging-in-Publication Data

2015937475

9780718030629

Printed in the United States of America

15 16 17 18 19 20 [RRD] 6 5 4 3 2 1

To Juanita Jean Siveright Moran
You left me too early in life, yet something tells me that you
would have loved this journey I've been on. Can't wait to
sit with you in the shadow of our King and introduce you
to so many who know about you through my story.

CONTENTS

PART ONE: The Problem

PART TWO: The Solution

FOREWORD

've known Roy Moran for several years. I'm not sure when our relationship started because he was cyberstalking me long before we met. When we finally met by phone, my thought was, *This guy is nuts!* But my wife reminded me that this is exactly what most people say about me. Our relationship has matured to weekends spent in skull sessions, lively discussions on many different topics, a willingness to call each other on our personal biases, a room in his house that he and his wife, Candy, insist is the David Watson room, and Roy sleeping on an air mattress in my game room and watching the Kansas City Royals play the final game of the 2014 World Series in the media room.

Our mutual nuttiness stems from different views of the same problem and very different responses to that problem: the churches we grew up in and the churches we led are very different from the church as revealed in the Bible. I took my longing to see an obedient, Bible-based church outside the church by starting Disciple-Making Movements that led to obedience-based churches in places where there were no existing churches. I started with a mostly clean slate.

Roy took the opposite, and much more difficult, approach. He worked within existing church structures and stretched them in extreme ways to cause change. He has often been a voice crying in the wilderness, but his is a voice that needs to be heard.

Spent Matches is a story we may not want to hear, but earnestly need to hear. The church is in trouble. It is not significantly changing lives, and certainly is no longer a major voice in Western culture. Membership in a church does not equate to allegiance to Christ, making it possible for a person to wear a cross, the symbol of Christ's sacrifice for our redemption, and to wantonly continue in the sin for which Christ died. There is statistically little difference in the behavior of church members and the behavior of those who never go to church. Why is this a reality?

The church is losing the battle for the hearts and minds of those who don't know Christ. Our relevance in modern society is dwindling, and our impact on those who call themselves Christian is limited. We have failed to produce disciple-making disciples and continue to hold form as more important than function and our history more important than our future. As long as we look good it doesn't seem to matter that there is a significant heart problem that is destroying us.

Roy Moran and his church, Shoal Creek, are on a journey to reverse this trend. Shoal Creek has embraced a lifestyle that shows people how to know God rather than simply know about God. They are active in attracting and in searching for those who want to know more about God and who want to know how to discover for themselves how to live in a deep relationship with God and a right relationship with people. They have moved from discipleship programs to multiplicative disciple-making.

Spent Matches is a road map for the modern church to discover how to make disciple-makers and have significant impact on families and communities. It will help you take a critical look at yourself and your church. It will show you some of the dead ends, as well as some of the highways to disciple-making disciples. It will lead you to becoming and developing self-feeding disciples who make self-feeding disciples. It will challenge you to fail forward quickly—learning from mistakes and endeavoring to never repeat them and finding success where none was apparent. It will push you to train, train, train; and to train in an adaptive way that meets the diversity of the urban setting.

Roy does not simply outline the problems of the modern church; he proposes solutions that are variable and scalable to your situation. This is not a one-size-fits-all book. It is a process-oriented book that will help you build your own solutions to the problems you face in your church. This book will not save you any time. It will pile the work on, but it will be meaningful work that will produce lasting results.

The practicality of *Spent Matches* will give you the starting points you need to make a difference in your ministry and your church. Approach it with prayer. Approach it with courage. Approach it with an open heart and mind. Let it hurt. Let it heal. Let it change your future.

Blessings!
David Watson
Coauthor of *Contagious Disciple-Making: Leading Others on a Journey of Discovery*

PREFACE

HOW TO READ THIS BOOK

This book may feel as if it is written by someone afflicted with Attention Deficit Disorder. However, bouncing back and forth between topics is by design. I've always felt people need to be reminded more than they need to be informed. I'm pretty sure someone famous said that, but I started to look it up and got distracted.

You may also notice that the nature of the subject matter here is difficult to cut into sections, a bit like dissecting a family pet. The process may be informative but the results are tragic. Exploring the vitality of the spiritual journey by rethinking Jesus' commands and the structure and form of the church, among others things, is a circular rather than linear trek. We pass the same way many times, but on an ever-deepening spiral of faith and action.

My hope is that you will read these words as a journal and not a manual. There is no recipe or formula contained in these pages, only the interaction between truth and reality. We hold the same truth, but we experience different realities. I want to encourage you to think beyond current forms and act to see Jesus' last command obeyed.

For some reason I always feel guilty if I start a book but don't finish it. I think it comes from an athletic background where I heard people say, "quitters never win" too many times. You have my permission not to read the entire book. Not all these chapters are for everyone. This is especially so if you find yourself outside the church looking in. Read what works for you and ignore the rest.

If you are a church-avoiding, spiritually dissatisfied person, not sure if this book is for you, let me give you a tip. Start at chapter 7, "The 7 Journeys: Moving from Analog to Digital Spirituality." If that intrigues you, move to chapter 9 to regain confidence that church can possibly be different.

Don't read this as a treatise defending a position or advocating a new departure from the norm. Try to view this instead as the ramblings and wonderings of an armchair historian, theologian, and biblical strategist. My hope is to antagonize you enough to ignite an exploration that helps you question the way you read the Bible, which then turns into an exploration that challenges the way you've always done things. Such an exploration can lead to a more effective accomplishment of Jesus' last command.

I turned sixty in 2014, what a year it was! I walked the Camino de Santiago, spent three weeks in Australia, played golf at the Old Course in St. Andrews, Scotland, met with pastors in Eastern Africa, and visited the Bhojpuri movement in Varanasi, India.

Sounds exciting, I know, but I would trade it all to see the Great Commission fulfilled in my lifetime. I've committed everything I have to seeing the Great Commission achieved. I hope in some way reading this book challenges you to join me.

PART ONE

THE PROBLEM

TELLING FAMILY SECRETS

EXPOSING THE WHOLE TRUTH
ABOUT THE SPREAD OF THE GOSPEL

I have been a follower of Christ since I was 17. Somewhere early in my spiritual journey, reaching those far from God became an abiding passion of mine. Please don't assume that I have a gift of evangelism, because I don't. I just have a passion for those far from God. I love to create environments in which people can safely approach a very dangerous message about life.

Despite not having the gift of evangelism, I have shared the gospel with others using the Four Spiritual Laws and drawn The Bridge to Life, popularized by the Navigators, on a napkin many times. I was certified as an Evangelism Explosion trainer and even developed an evangelism training program called Lifestyle Evangelism Outreach.

I have been involved in 3 church plants and was on staff at 1 traditional church. A graduate of Dallas Seminary, I haven't strayed far from my theological roots. I still believe the Bible is the final authority in all matters. Despite my theological orthodoxy, you may find that my methodologies stretch beyond your comfort level.

This chapter isn't a legal brief proving conclusively that my method of sharing the gospel is valid. The evidence (if you can call it that) is circumstantial at best. All I want is for you to hear a different story, take a look at the other side of the numbers, and be thought-ful about what this all means. I am merely asking that you give me a hearing. Take a different look. You don't have to accept my con-clusions, but you'll benefit from hearing a new perspective. I believe that if we know there is another side of the coin and work to engage both sides, then we might be open to doing things differently.

Jim Collins, in his book *Good to Great,* describes meeting Admi-ral James Stockdale (USN ret.), who was the highest ranking US Naval prisoner at the Hanoi Hilton, the North Vietnamese prison for American military during the Vietnam War. When asked which prisoners didn't survive their long ordeal, Stockdale said without hes-itation, "Optimists." The prisoners' use of milestones such as Thanks-giving, Christmas, and New Years to build expectations for the date of their release became their worst enemy. The rise and fall of hope led to loss of hope and, for some, loss of life.

Stockdale told Collins, "This is a very important lesson. You must never confuse faith that you will prevail in the end—which you can never afford to lose—with the discipline to confront the most brutal facts of your current reality, whatever they might be."[1] This is a les-son, now referred to as the Stockdale Paradox, church leaders need to learn.

Pointing out the truth regarding the church is often deemed criti-cal, negative, and unspiritual. Therefore, Christians tend to spin bru-tal facts in a positive way. Being positive and encouraging is certainly an attribute to be desired, but when it masks reality, we become like Stockdale's optimists!

The leaders of the church today are guilty of overusing optimism. They may do so under the guise of casting vision or to shelter the church from the truth. Our modern aversion to motivating by guilt keeps us from maturing in our skills at handling negative information and actions. Overreliance on optimism colors our understanding of the growth of the church and its impact and hinders us from devel-oping the passion to question current strategies.

We love to extol life-changing stories that happen around us. No doubt there are many amazing stories of God's intervention and transformation in our world. I don't want to devalue what is happening. But there is a bigger picture, a global picture. If seen, it might change the way we feel about how we bring the message of Jesus to this world.

The defense mechanism of relying on anecdotal/local stories rather than confronting brutal, global facts is an ingrained habit. It robs us of learning and adjusting our strategies to be more effective. We tend to focus on the data, small as it may be, that confirms the conclusions that we want to draw.

This is much like the story of the man who thought he was dead. His wife was going so crazy trying to convince him to the contrary that she had to go to the doctor for her own health. When the doctor found out what was causing her stress, he asked to see the husband each day for a week. Every day at the doctor's office, the man learned about anatomy and physiology.

> We tend to focus on the data, small as it may be, that confirms the conclusions that we want to draw.

He learned about the vascular system and blood pressure. He discovered how this closed system always has pressure due to the work of the heart muscle. He saw that when the system is punctured, blood comes pouring out. Finally on Friday, the doctor had the wife come in with her husband. He asked the man, "Do dead men bleed?" The man explained articulately that dead men don't bleed because of the pressure in the vascular system run by the heart.

Upon hearing this, the doctor picked up a big hypodermic needle and thrust it into the man's arm. He immediately started bleeding profusely. The wife was appalled that her doctor would do such a thing. But her husband grabbed his arm and screamed, "Doc, Doc, dead men do bleed! The doctor hung his head in dismay.

The man's belief that he was dead was so strong that it controlled even his own experience of bleeding and led to the erroneous conclusion that dead men bleed. This man was stricken with "paradigm paralysis," a concept Joel Barker made famous.[2] Not even information that proved him wrong would change his mind. He was convinced of his conclusion, and the facts weren't going to mess that up.

PARADIGMS: FRIEND OR FOE

Paradigm paralysis almost brought the Swiss watchmaking industry to extinction. The Swiss dominated the world of watchmaking for many years. They were constantly making improvements, inventing the minute and second hands and self-winding watches. In 1968, they owned 60 percent of the watch market and 80 percent of the profits. Yet over the next 25 years their market share would collapse to just 10 percent. Between 1969 and 1971, 50,000 watchmakers—80 percent of the watchmaking workforce—lost their jobs. What happened?

While they invented the electronic quartz watch, they turned their proverbial noses up at it because it was battery powered and, therefore, didn't have the finely crafted mechanisms of traditional Swiss watches. Their paradigm blinded them to consumer satisfaction with an accurate, inexpensive timepiece. The Japanese were more than willing to take the design; they put digital watches on so many wrists that the Swiss could no longer compete.[3] Failing to allow information into your decision-making mechanisms can be lethal. Paradigm paralysis can be fatal!

Thinking is much like working with a spreadsheet. We input data to calculate a conclusion. Unfortunately, we often neglect to include a column for new data. Paradigm paralysis begins when we refuse to put new data in our spreadsheet. A flexible, growing mind opens up another column on the spreadsheet for the new data, even if it is confusing or doesn't fit neatly. Keeping it in view stops the filtering process of accepting only data that confirms our beliefs.

We use confirmation bias to support conclusions we've already drawn about our effectiveness in expanding Jesus' mission. Unfortunately, our conclusions may not be based on careful deliberations, but are instead reached through quick Google searches and faintly remembered quotations from things we have read. Often, local, anecdotal stories substitute for global, brutal facts, thus confirming our bias that we are doing just fine with the spread of Jesus' mission.

To avoid succumbing to paradigm paralysis, let's take a stroll through the history of the good news as it began in Palestine and moved throughout the world. Even if you aren't a numbers person, a fresh and clear understanding of what has happened and where we are headed will give you a basis for deciding whether the strategies we have in play today are effective.

The question guiding me through this minefield is: "What needs to be done?" When I focus on what needs to be done, I am driven by Jesus' command to go to all people groups. That is a daunting task and dangerous to put in our field of view. It can be, and often is, discouraging. So, instead of keeping the faith that we will prevail, we hang on to optimism that what we have been doing will be enough.

I have an irrational passion: I don't know how it developed, but God continues to feed it. I keep asking that question, "What needs to be done?" This passion has driven me to look at the numbers with a different point of view that some might call a negative or critical spirit. I like to think of it as confronting the brutal facts. I believe wholeheartedly that Jesus will build His church, wash it with His word, and present it holy and blameless one day. But that doesn't keep me from looking into the face of our current situation.

When throwing numbers around, we need to heed a statement attributed to Mark Twain, "Facts are stubborn but statistics are more pliable." Turning the numbers around and around to make sure we see all sides and engage all the implications that the facts are giving us prevents us from creating optimistic blindness. Let's take a look at just what the growth of the church has been over the centuries to make sure that we are clear about how we've carried out Jesus' final command.

THE GROWTH OF JESUS' MOVEMENT

At the end of the first century AD, there were 180 million people on the earth and about 1.8 million of them were Christ-followers. There is no doubt that growth from 120 (Acts 1:15) to 1.8 million people in 70 years is impressive. But that 1.8 million represented only 1 percent of the earth's population. It also represented the 99 percent, 178 million people who did not know Christ.[4]

Often, the fourth century AD is seen as critical because of Emperor Constantine's flirtation with Christianity. The sincerity of his conversion to Christianity is a battle ground for theologically inclined church historians. Let's ask the question, however: What does the spread of Jesus' message look like after?

In AD 300, 8 percent of the 190 million inhabitants of earth were Christian or about 14.3 million people. That is better than a tenfold increase in the church in 200 years. Certainly news worth celebrating, but it also means that 175 million faced a Christ-less eternity.

Constantine is accused of perverting Christianity by making it the "official" religion and allowing property ownership by local assemblies, thus moving the church from homes to owned buildings. The numbers show that Constantine's efforts between AD 300 and 400 almost doubled the number of Christians, growing to 25 million. Still though, that accounts for only 13 percent of the global population.

Is it possible to maintain the joy of seeing millions of new people relating to God as their heavenly Father and conversely mourning that fact that 100 times that many are headed to a Christ-less eternity? That is what it means to confront the brutal facts. Jesus' parables of loss in Luke 15 represent both passion for those who are lost and joy in those who are found. I can't imagine a God who doesn't live eternally with the joy and angst of both.

As the world's population remains relatively steady through AD 600, the number of Christians rises to almost 40 million, or 22 percent. Constantine didn't seem to have a significant detrimental effect on the expansion of the good news. Despite the addition of 27 million people to the roles of the universal church, we are still left with 140 million people without Jesus as an advocate.

Moving on, the Middle Ages weren't good to the world population. By AD 1000 only 80 million people had been added to the earth, bringing the total population to 264 million, yet Christians accounted for only 16.9 percent, or 44.6 million. Only 4 million people were added to the church—not a significant increase over a 400-year period!

By 1500, 18 percent of the world's population, 423 million, were Christian. That is almost double the percentage of Christians from the year 1000. But our ability to penetrate every people group begins to struggle as the population begins to rise. Although the number of Christians has risen from 1.8 million in year 1000, to 75 million in year 1500, the number of people facing a Christ-less eternity has also risen. It doesn't take Einstein to know the alternate number of 18 percent is 82 percent. This represents 346 million who are without Christ—an alarming number of people.

> **Jesus' parables of loss in Luke 15 represent both passion for those who are lost and joy in those who are found.**

The twentieth century saw significant movement in all of these numbers. The world grew to over 1.6 billion people, and Christianity penetrated 34.5 percent of that population, or over a half a billion Christ followers. It was a period of unprecedented growth caused by travel, trade, and exploration. The gospel took a ride along with trade and commerce. This might be called the "Golden Age of

Christianity," because we have yet to achieve any more significant penetration than seen during this time.

Bradley A. Coon is a research assistant at the Center for the Study of Global Christianity at Gordon Conwell Theological Seminary. He put into words what the twentieth century delivered, "Christianity as a whole has grown at roughly the same average annual rate as the population (1.32 percent and 1.37 percent respectively). This means that in AD 2000, the percentage of Christians in the world was nearly the same as in AD 1900."[5]

While the world's population skyrocketed from 1.6 billion in 1900, to 6.1 billion people in 2000, Christians remained only a third of the world's people. Granted, 33 percent of 6 billion is 2 billion people, something we can (and should) celebrate, but in 1900, there were about a billion people who were headed for a Christ-less eternity. Today there are upward of 4 billion in that category, a figure that should cause us to rethink why we are losing our effectiveness.

Despite the gains that are worthy of celebrating, the loss is unsettling! It is two sides of the same coin. We can focus on the growth of the church with blind optimism, or we can choose to pay attention to our inability to effectively reach a rapidly expanding population. Here's a third possibility: we can confront the brutal facts in Stockdale Paradox style and begin to explore why we have become increasingly ineffective at spreading the good news. Then we can entertain different strategies to reach fast-growing populations and areas untouched by the message of Jesus.

INSIDE THE NUMBERS

Despite what might be couched as phenomenal growth over a period of 2,000 years—120 followers of Christ to 2.3 billion, the largest percentage of gains in those numbers is due to births, not evangelism or conversion. We are increasing in the total number of people who claim Jesus as their Redeemer and Leader, but the rest of the story needs to be told. More and more people are facing a

Christ-less eternity than ever before. We are not gaining ground equivalent with our population growth. The other side of the 2.3 billion is at least 4.7 billion without the hope of Jesus.

Let's dig a little deeper into the numbers. Annually, 55 million new people are counted as Christian. When we unpack that number, we realize that 42 million of those are children born to Christian families, while only 19 million are people who become new followers of Jesus,[6] otherwise known as *converts*. In and of itself, 19 million is a lot of people, but when viewed as a percentage of the global population, it is just .27 of 1 percent! Think about this: God uses 2.3 billion followers of Christ to bring 19 million of the 7 billion people in the world into the family of God. Can we be satisfied with these results? If we bear the spirit of the story of the lost coin, lost sheep, and lost son in Luke 15, shouldn't there be a spirit of "*by* any means necessary" to change these numbers?

Gordon Conwell's Center for the Study of Global Christianity (CSGC) calculated the cost of baptizing one person globally in 2014 at $753,000. All the money contributed to expanding the mission of Jesus around the globe, divided by the number of people converted to Christianity gives us this figure. We can all agree that you can't put a price on a human soul, but when our strategies cost this much, we must pause and wonder whether we should reconsider how we are attempting to reach the world. Is this all we have? Even if we could afford to fund our current strategies, they just aren't effective. CSGC forecasts that by 2025, the cost of baptizing one person globally will rise to $1.4 million.[7] In 2001, two researchers calculated the cost of baptizing one person in the United States at $1.5 million.[8] That is exponential growth in the cost of spreading the gospel. Is this what Jesus intended? Even if we could get Jesus' followers to double or triple—or you pick the factor—giving toward world discipleship, it wouldn't matter. More of the same is not the solution.

Even if we could afford to fund our current strategies, they just aren't effective.

Roland Allen, a missiologist, sounded the warning this way:

It is, I suppose, now almost universally admitted that we cannot hope, by multiplication of missionaries, to reach the vast populations of China, India and Africa, not to mention the rest of the world, nor to cover the whole of these great areas with mission stations, still less to provide mission schools and hospitals sufficient to supply their needs. The demands made upon us by our present missions for money and support tend rather to increase than to diminish from year to year. . . . Surely there must be an end to this process some time. If we are to admit that the more successful the work of establishing a church the greater is the obligation of the home church to sustain its various needs, it is not difficult to foresee disaster. [9]

Allen's book was first published in 1927! Did anyone hear him? And still no one is listening?

Another caveat on the numbers we have been trudging through is the definition of *Christian*. A popular and respected research institution defines the word this way: "followers of Jesus Christ of all kinds; all traditions and confessions; and all degrees of commitment."[10] Definitions in this arena expose bias and judgment. So, to be clear, we have been talking about the word *Christian* in the broadest of terms. If we confined ourselves to evangelicals, then the total numbers would shrink from 2.3 billion to 400 million followers of Jesus worldwide, or 5.7 percent of the world's population. The situation worsens the more we unpack the meaning of the numbers.

Researchers looking to bolster the spirits of the global flock are getting their exercise as the true numbers are beginning to be exposed. Ed Stetzer, president of Lifeway Research, in a *USA Today* article, attempts to refute the premise that Christianity is on its way to extinction in the United States, "Those cultural Christians are becoming 'nones' [people with no religious label]." He goes on to say, "Christianity is not collapsing, but it is being clarified."[11] And he is spot on! We are beginning to get a clear picture that the numbers representing Christians in the world today are even worse than we once thought.

The Joshua Project, which counts unreached people groups (UPGs), reports 6,974 UPGs (42 percent of all people groups), representing 2.9 billion of the world's 7.03 billion people (41.8 percent). Not only have these people not been converted, the mission of Jesus has yet to reach them. They neither have the hope of Jesus nor know of Him.

Despite almost 40 years of emphasis on unreached people groups, many still have no church-planting work of any kind among them. Others might have had such work in the past, but do not currently. Such groups are sometimes identified as unengaged unreached people groups (UUPGs), and many mission strategists are seeking to move churches and mission agencies beyond adopting a people to actively engaging them in actual church planting work.[12]

We need to have a "burning platform" mentality.

It is not that we've completely failed, but the unfinished task is of such serious proportion that we need to have a "burning platform" mentality. (The "burning platform" metaphor comes from the Piper Alpha oil-drilling disaster in the North Sea, the worst disaster in the history of North Sea oil exploration, where 166 crew and 2 rescuers lost their lives. Superintendent Andy Mochan survived the disaster by leaping from the burning platform into the oil-fired frozen ocean. He knew he had 20 minutes at the most to survive in the sea but when he looked at his options he said, "It was fry or jump, so I jumped."[13])

As we fall further and further behind in reaching the world's population, someone needs to sound the alarm, as Roland Allen did in his generation. Our platform is on fire. We can stay on the platform, hoping to survive, or we can jump like Andy did and change our effectiveness at obeying Jesus' last command. Jumping means opening our minds to what God is up to around the world; it means becoming aware of the assumptions driven by our culture that we have brought to the pages of the Bible. Learning to reread the Bible without our culturally biased lenses and seeing what Jesus was up to in the first century could lead us to reducing the alarming proportions of people headed to hell.

DARK CLOUDS BEHIND EVERY STATISTIC

My wife and kids will tell you that my favorite meal is a bunch of appetizers. In fact one of my daughters-in-law once asked my son, "Does your family eat any real food?" I love a variety of tastes in small portions. So I want to continue to put an array of statistics on the table to help us see just how difficult a situation we are in. I am arguing that the church is becoming increasingly ineffective, not extinct. I would love for us to open the door to explore more strategy options than we currently pursue.

GLOBAL FACTORS

The fact that more Christians live in the Global South (Asia, Africa, Latin America, and Oceania) than the Global North (Europe and Northern America) certainly sounds exciting, but this may not represent a positive trend. It may say more about the Global North than it does the Global South! It could possibly be a harbinger of what is to come for the South. They may be following in the footsteps of the Global North. Are we looking at the golden age of the Global South today? Since Christianity is not keeping pace with global population growth, we may just be rearranging the proverbial chairs on the deck of the *Titanic* while the ship slowly sinks. The Global North is taking on water; is the Global South getting ready to follow suit?

Another disturbing fact relates to the wealth that exists in the Christian community north and south of the equator. Even though 60 percent of Christians live in the Global South, they control only

17 percent of the wealth of Christianity.[14] The church in the Global South is beginning to ramp up the sending of missionaries, some even to the Global North. With only 16 percent of the wealth, will the current, expensive models of gospel outreach become a burden too heavy to bear?

US REALITIES

If we focus in on the West, we know that Europe already exists in a post-Christian state, which is reflected in the single-digit percentages of church attendance. While the United States has been the primary funder and exporter of the Christian message in the twenty-first century, today the United States is close on the heels of Europe in its percentage of church attendance. From 1990 to 2006, the US population grew by almost 60 million, yet church attendance increased by half a million.[15]

You would be hard-pressed to find a state in the United States that has shown an increase in church attendance in the last decade. Even states such as California, Texas, and Georgia—in which megachurches serve as models for many new church starts—couldn't report positive figures for church attendance in the last decade.

Younger churches experience more conversions than older churches. But when we expose just how much effect these new churches have, we understand that it is insignificant in the grand scheme. I am not saying that even a single conversion is insignificant. Even one conversion is worth celebrating, as Jesus taught us in Luke 15. But a fact that surprised me is that until recently, more churches closed each year than were started.[16]

Of the estimated 400,000 US churches, only 3.5 percent are effective at expanding Jesus' kingdom, meaning that fewer than 4 churches out of 100 maintain a conversion ratio of 20:1 or better. When you consider that the nation's population is now 300 million, if only 3.5 percent of churches are healthy in the area of conversion growth, then there's only 1 healthy church for every 21,400 persons in the United States![17]

Even though it is difficult to keep all the statistics straight, it becomes increasingly discouraging when you see them together:

- Of the 350 thousand churches in the United States, less than 1 percent is growing by conversion growth."[18]

- Globally, even though we see 19 million conversions each year, we also see 19 million defectors from the Christian faith.[19]

- In America, 9 out of 10 churches are declining or growing at a pace slower than the rate of their communities.[20]

- The average established church declines by 2 percent per year.[21]

- Evangelical churches aren't baptizing nearly enough people to keep up with population growth. Among the white middle class, church has been their political, economic, and social base; they rarely make a true adult convert. The great majority of people being baptized in evangelical churches are already baptized Christians and children.[22]

Christine Wicker in *The Fall of the Evangelical Nation: The Surprising Crisis Inside the Church* concludes:

Evangelical Christianity in America is dying. The great evangelical movements of today are not a vanguard. They are a remnant, unraveling at every edge. Look at it any way you like: Conversions. Baptisms. Membership. Retention. Participation. Giving. Attendance. Religious literacy. Effect on culture. All are down and dropping. It's no secret. Even as evangelical forces trumpet their purported political and social victories, insiders are anguishing about their great losses, fearing what the future holds. Nobody knows what to do about it. A lot of people can't believe it. No wonder. The idea that evangelicals are taking over America is one of the greatest publicity scams in history, a perfect coup accomplished by savvy politicos and religious leaders, who understand media weaknesses and exploit them brilliantly.[23]

She is right. That is the family secret. There was a moment in history when we wielded political power, and we were dubbed the Moral Majority. Today, we are not the majority anymore, if we ever were. In fact, our numbers are small and getting smaller.

To make matters worse, we are not even moral. Our divorce rate is the same as the general populations whether you look at "Born Agains" or "Evangelicals."[24] When Yale researchers studied the 12 million "True Love Waits" pledge takers, they found that 88 percent of them had sex before they were married, thus violating their pledges.[25]

Whether it's sexuality, media use, racism, or wealth; when measured together, the people who claim to follow Jesus don't seem to agree with His views about many of these issues. Michael Horton laments, "Gallup and Barna hand us survey after survey demonstrating that evangelical Christians are as likely to embrace lifestyles every bit as hedonistic, materialistic, self-centered, and sexually immoral as the world in general."[26] When seen individually, we can minimize or compartmentalize these statistics. But once you put them all together, even the faithful begin to quiver.

MONEY MATTERS

Statistics related to church giving are disheartening. Take, for instance, generational factors: 69 percent of all charitable contributions come from those 49 years old and older.[27] Current life expectancy rates suggest that the 49 year-old donor has 30 years to live. Imagine if almost 70 percent of the wealth that the church has learned to operate on disappears in the next 30 years. No doubt the megachurches will feel the brunt of this loss as they attempt to pay large staffs and keep running the plants and facilities they've grown accustomed to.

The giving habits of the younger generations shrink in alarming numbers as you go down the chronological ladder. Crowd funding, text giving, and all the new ways invented to get younger generations to discover a generosity gene aren't plugging the leak. Books such as John Dickerson's *The Great Evangelical Recession*[28] chronicle in detail this coming collapse, and it is not a pretty sight to behold.

Solomon warns us in Proverbs 22:3, "Prudent people see trouble coming and hide, but the naive walk right into it and take a beating." History is littered with harbingers who cried out and were ignored, the most recent being the many financial experts who warned banks about the subprime mortgage investments that helped send the world into the worst recession of modern times. Many leaders stood by helpless, captive to their conventional thinking, watching the world markets crumble.

I sense we are on a burning platform. We have cultivated fig trees that are not producing the fruit Jesus expects. We can either stick our heads in the sand and pretend we are on the track that Jesus intended, or we can confront the brutal facts without giving up our ultimate objectives and see if God might be saying something we have yet to hear.

Our strategies are too expensive and too bureaucratic to move at the speed of the population growth around the world. We don't have the forethought to fund "incubators" that bring together the best and the brightest of Jesus' disciple-makers to develop and test new ways to reach mega-cities, extend the gospel to the Unengaged Unreached People Groups, and develop flexible, biblical models to extend the reach of the good news to the ends of the earth.

MORE THAN MONEY

We are facing an ever-increasing number of obstacles beyond just money. Political barriers create roadblocks to traditional ways of evangelizing and church planting. We are experiencing an inability to recruit and train a new generation to respond as the Greatest

Generation and even Baby Boomers did to historical models of mission. Accelerated urbanization will continue as more of the world lives in the complex landscapes of cities, further eroding the relational potential for the good news.

Howard Hendricks was a formative mentor in my life. He used stories to communicate truth better than anyone I know. One of Hendricks's famous stories recalls a sales meeting of the Fido Dog Food company. The sales manager mounted the podium in cheerleader fashion and shouted, "Who's got the best sales force in the dog food world?" The crowd responded, "WE DO!"

Again, he shouted, "Who's got the best dog food products in the world?" Again the salesmen respond, WE DO!" Then with a change of tone, the sales leader asked, "Then why are we 16 out of 17 in sales for dog food?" One lone voice from the middle of the crowd said, "Because dogs don't like us." There are some truths worth facing to change the status quo.

> **The fundamental issue lies in our inability to overcome at least a century of moral failure.**

Despite the hip, cool, culturally relevant methods that churches have employed, the fact remains that people who don't go to church don't like people who do. We've created a church culture that reeks of intolerance and self-righteousness. Besides that, we are largely white, middle-to-upper-middle class, and live in the suburbs. Despite all of our modernizations of the concept we call *church*—crazy cool architecture, use of modern music, media drenched church meetings, meeting in houses, incarnating ourselves in a poverty-stricken neighborhood, or slinging multisite venues closer to where people live—the fundamental issue lies in our inability to overcome at least a century of moral failure.

Whether that moral failure is being on the wrong side of slavery issues, failing to live out God's heart on race issues, not engaging the AIDS crisis appropriately, defrosting our attitudes toward poverty, failing to find a way to express being created male and female in a way that values both male and female appropriately, or the public moral collapse of evangelical media darlings in every decade that I've lived in, we the church have an image problem. There is no public relations firm that can help! The truth seems to be that non-church-going people just don't like us.

Worldwide, we've exported a kind of Christianity that has stood silent and even participated in some of the worst tragedies in modern times. Rwanda was considered to be one of the most "Christian" countries in the world before 1994. Yet with 80–90 percent of its citizens identifying as Christian, this country was the site of some of the worst genocidal atrocities in Africa—800,000 men, women, and children slaughtered in the name of tribal domination. If the statistics are true about the Christians in Rwanda, most of those fighting in the name of a tribe also identified as Christian. Somehow the good news that reached Rwanda didn't go as deep as the tribal identities developed in the homes of the Tutsi and Hutu.[29]

Back in the United States, our troubles are not only with the present but also with the future. The trends are so dire it threatens our ability to hope. The number of Americans who do not identify with any religion continues to grow at an alarming rate. One-fifth of the US public and a third of adults under 30 are religiously unaffiliated today, the highest percentages ever reported by the Pew Research Center. From 2010 through 2014 alone, the unaffiliated have increased from just over 15 percent to just under 20 percent of all US adults. This includes more than 13 million self-described atheists and agnostics (nearly 6 percent of the US public), as well as nearly 33 million people who say they have no particular religious affiliation (14 percent).

In 2008, Pew Research reported that 20–30 year olds attend church at half the rate of their parents and a quarter of the rate of their grandparents.[30] Depending on the researcher, between 60 percent and 88 percent of *churched* youth will not attend church in their twenties.[31]

LISTEN TO JESUS

Is there hope? I believe there is. I believe Jesus wants to build His church, and He wants us to disciple the world. The reason we find ourselves in this predicament pertains to our ever-increasing desire to add complexity to the simplicity that Jesus left us with. He wants us to pay attention to what He has said.

I find hope in listening to what God is doing in India and other countries in the East. In Habakkuk 1:5, God says, "Take a look at the nations and watch *what happens*! / You will be shocked and amazed. / For in your days, I am doing a work, / a work you'll never believe even if someone tells you *plainly*!" This is God speaking, not Roy Moran. Is it time to open up that column in our spreadsheets and let some new data sit there until the Spirit is able to get our eyes open and our hearts softened?

Jesus wants to build His church, but when we confront the brutal facts, we are in bad shape. It should cause us to rethink why, how, and what we are doing. It is time to wipe the whiteboard clean and go back to the Gospels and ask, "What exactly did Jesus say and what should we do?"

For instance, Jesus didn't say, "Go plant churches." He said "Go make disciples." We seem to have jumped right over Jesus and gone straight to Paul, building our methodologies off the apostolic movement of the gospel from Jerusalem to Antioch and beyond. The results of these journeys were churches, but a closer analysis of Paul's activities reveals that he, too, focused on making disciples. He told Timothy exactly what he should be about—making "disciple-making" disciples (2 Tim. 2:2). It is clear throughout history that you don't always get disciples when you plant churches; but if you make disciple-making disciples, you always get the church as Jesus intended it.

As I write, Adam Lewis Green closed the third most successful Kickstarter campaign to date. Green's project, *Bibliotheca*, was conceived as a way to print the Bible in a more readable form. Among the hundreds of innovative, techno savvy Kickstarter projects out there, who would have guessed a Bible project would succeed wildly beyond expectation? *Bibliotheca* doesn't contain pictures, media links, or even a modern translation to bolster perceived value. Using the American Standard Version of 1901 with some changes (such as *you* for *thou*), *Bibliotheca* reads like stories because all the chapter and verse numbers and other "helps" have been stripped away. *Bibliotheca*'s success proves once again that our job is not to add to the message of Jesus but to make it accessible to all of God's people. It is not that people don't want to explore Jesus, God, and the Bible. They are afraid of those who have gathered around His mission. We can reverse that trend by sticking to the methods that got us here.

TIME FOR CHANGE

Here's my agenda, plain and simple: there could be a different way of doing things. The question is whether we are open to exploring it. The current strategies in play today, evangelism and church planting, have been somewhat effective but are decreasing in their effectiveness. Could it be time to reread the Bible and put our culture bias in plain view? Is it time to sacrifice some sacred cows to see the gospel set free and move freely through cul-de-sacs, across closed borders, and into wounded hearts?

Many of the numbers examined here represent what is happening in the United States. Apart from South America and Africa, the rest of the world either leads or follows close behind the predicament in the United States.

The mantra "Church planting is the best methodology of evangelism under the sun"[32] still guides the minds of the leaders of the Christian movement. Despite the fact that we are seeing more and more people on a track to hell, we continue to plow money and people into ineffective strategies. Turn the numbers any way you want, and you will still get the same results.

We exist in an age when the Western church has more resources than at any time in history. Yet despite the wealth of Western Christians, more people are hell-bound than any other time in history. Shouldn't we just pause and ask some hard questions? Are we so deeply committed to our cultural interpretations of the Bible that we can't peel away our cultural scales and understand Jesus' last words to His followers?

Data shows that every one of us lives in an under-reached, if not an unreached, area. What is currently called the church is not going to get the job done. Creating more churches like the ones we already have flies in the face of reason. The cost of church planting alone is an unreasonable answer to how we are going to reach any major metropolitan area in the world.

It is easy to lose the mental discipline of the Stockdale Paradox when talking about the progress of the gospel through history, especially when coupled with the immaturity and ineffectiveness of the church. All too often, Christians confuse confronting the brutal facts with lack of faith. It is possible both to believe that Jesus was true and faithful when He said that the gates of hell will not prevail against His church and to admit the poor progress of the church through the centuries, not to mention the lack of maturity among those who call themselves Christians!

We are on a burning platform, and it is time to act. We can be like the folks on the *Titanic*, who danced the night away as the water flooded the decks below, or we can learn from the passengers of United Flight #93. On September 11, 2001, there were 4 American passenger aircraft hijacked. Three of them reached their intended targets, the World Trade Towers and the Pentagon. The fourth plane crashed in a field in southern Pennsylvania. Passengers of

We are on a burning platform, and it is time to act.

United Flight #93, upon learning of the fate of other hijacked aircrafts, thought theirs might be on the way to the White House.

They perceived a burning platform. Either act or sit by and be
part of the worst tragedy in American history. They jumped, organized themselves into a militia, and attempted to overpower the
hijackers. As passengers made an attempt to regain control of the
aircraft, United Flight #93 crashed into an unpopulated field in rural
Pennsylvania. Everyone on board (except for the hijackers) are celebrated to this day as American heroes.

How much do we love the mission that Jesus gave us? Is it worth
the sacrifice of our lives to stop the trends we are experiencing
today? Are we willing to expose our inflexible misread of the Bible
and rethink our methods? Would we be willing to keep asking the
question, "What needs to be done?" and not default to the cop-out,
"I'll just do what I can do"?

THE GREAT COMMISSION

PUTTING THE *GREAT* BACK INTO JESUS' LAST COMMAND

¹⁶The eleven disciples, having spoken to the Marys, headed to Galilee, to the mountain where they were to meet Jesus. ¹⁷When the disciples saw Jesus there, many of them fell down and worshiped, as Mary and the other Mary had done. But a few hung back. They were not sure (and who can blame them?). ¹⁸Jesus came forward and addressed *His beloved disciples*. The disciples don't know what to think or how to act. Nothing like this has ever happened before.

Jesus: I am here speaking with all the authority of God, *who has commanded Me to give you this commission*: ¹⁹Go out and make disciples in all the nations. Ceremonially wash them through baptism in the name of the *triune God*: Father, Son, and Holy Spirit. ²⁰Then disciple them. *Form them in the practices and postures that* I have taught you, and show them how to follow the commands I have laid down for you. And I will be with you, day after day, to the end of the age.

—Matthew 28:16–20

Admittedly, the title *Great Commission* is not in the biblical text of Matthew 28:18–20, but it is a universally acknowledged title for this passage. Few, if any, theological pundits would pigeonhole this text as a command given exclusively to the group gathered on the mountain the day Jesus spoke and not to all followers of Christ to come after them.

Think with me for a moment. Read the statement below and decide whether you agree or disagree:

> The Great Commission subordinates every other command in the Bible so that all of Jesus' teaching should be understood in light of it and, therefore, it is the prime directive for followers of Christ until His return.

Is the Great Commission really that great? Why do we call it the "Great Commission," if there are other things in the Bible that are of equal if not greater value? What about the commands Jesus called the "greatest and first commandment" (Matt. 22:36–40)? Do we dare subordinate this command to the commands of Matthew 28:18–20, when Jesus Himself said that all the law and the prophets hang on loving God and loving others?

Let's push the pause button for a moment and travel through Matthew 28:16–20 to make sure we see eye to eye on what Jesus says, then we'll revisit this tension.

The ancient philosopher Epictetus cautioned that it is impossible for a man to learn what he thinks he already knows. I have been guilty of overlooking the obvious because I presume to be familiar with a subject or passage. We need to be careful that we read, not with the lenses of our culture or theological mentors, but with fresh eyes—eyes that long to see what Jesus said despite the challenges it brings to us personally or theologically.

To feel the texture of that day on a mountain in Galilee, we must begin reading in verse 16. Here we find who was gathered to hear Jesus' last command. At least eleven disciples were gathered. These eleven disciples are often referred to historically as the apostles. The meaning of that title, *apostle*, or "sent one," becomes obvious as we read the passage.

It is impossible for a man to learn what he thinks he already knows.

Matthew gave us insight into the spiritual temperature of these eleven men; some προσεκύνησαν (worshiped or bowed down) but others ἐδίστασαν (hung back or doubted.) When Jesus appeared, people had two distinct, presumably visible, reactions to His presence.

I am guessing by Matthew's use of terms that it was clear who was who. Maybe there were specific looks on their faces. One group knew they were in the presence of Jesus who was dead and was now alive. Another group wasn't sure if this were real.

What would you do if you were Jesus? The team in which you've invested more than three years of your life, the team you are hoping will change the world, the team that is Plan A (with no Plan B in sight), the team that represents all you have to show for three years of work, shows serious signs of faith decay. It would seem the perfect time for a workshop or seminar to teach them, remind them, challenge them about recent history before speaking of responsibilities; time to retrench and save what you can of what might seem like a pitiful situation.

However, nothing of the sort took place. Matthew simply said some worshiped, some doubted. Jesus didn't exhibit any sense of alarm indicating this was out of the ordinary or unusual. He was quite comfortable with a team that didn't have it all together. In fact, He was comfortable commissioning people who not only lacked complete faith but were confirmed doubters.

We need to feel this scene: Jesus is about to entrust His mission to people who are not yet believers. In fact, reading ahead to the first chapter of the book of Acts, the question Jesus is asked, presumably by some of these same people, indicates that they are still quite clueless as to what Jesus is up to. Forty days earlier they were told to go to the entire world's population, and now they are asking if Jesus is going to set up a monarchy in Israel (Acts 1:6). They are clueless!

Despite the fact that worshipers and doubters were present, Jesus didn't separate the group into haves and have-nots, or even leaders and followers. He made no distinction based on what these people brought to the table. Whether they doubted or worshiped, they were treated as equals by Jesus. He was banking on both groups being able to carry out His mission.

Quite the opposite happens today in our discipleship programs. We attempt to fill disciples' minds with knowledge so they are qualified to travel with a life-changing message. Only then do we release them to make new disciples, to become "disciplers."

Here is the scene—the God of the universe spends three years with a group of people who couldn't be elected as elders, bishops, deacons, and possibly not even ushers in the typical church today. He commissions confirmed doubters as well as worshipers to take a message of hope and healing to the ends of the earth.

CHANGING OUR MINDS ABOUT WHO IS ABLE

I might seem to belabor this point, but the importance will be clear when we talk about how the rapid multiplication of disciples can take place. There is a paradigm shift needed that many are incapable of making because of the theological box we've painted ourselves in. The critical question we need to ask is, "Who is capable of making disciples?" Let's look to Jesus for our example and answer.

Jesus had been with, invested in, and spiritually challenged these folks. For three years His disciples watched, listened to, and interacted with Him. But in the presence of the greatest disciple-maker ever to exist, they were still deficient in their ability to know and trust Him. But Jesus' plan to deploy them wasn't gauged on their knowledge, redeemed state, or ability to trust.

Undaunted, Jesus continued, after His resurrection, to invest in a mixed group of worshipers and doubters. Jesus said all authority was given to Him, from one end of the universe to the other. In other words, there is no place that exists that Jesus does not have the last say. He can do or undo anything!

This is the first time during Jesus' presence on earth that He pulled rank. Up to this point, He may have exerted His power via miracles or insightful questioning, but he did not directly assert His position of prominence in the universe. He was here to do the Father's bidding. But now, He revealed that the Father had given Him unrestricted power in what is seen—earth, and what is unseen—heaven. In classic Hebrew phrasing, He was letting His followers know that His authority extended to as far as is possible one way, earth, and the other way, heaven, and to everything in between.

On the front end of this encounter on the mountain, Jesus asserted His position of authority in the universe. In light of His recent death and resurrection, His statement was essentially that no irredeemable harm could come to the apostles because Jesus controls everything. His promise on the back end is equally important.

The message to everyone, those on their faces and those backing up, can be summarized as, "I am in charge, therefore I can be trusted." The appeal is to the will and not the mind, an appeal coming from a Hebrew mind-set and not a Greek one (read more about this in chapter 4). What was about to be said didn't depend on how they felt or what they knew but on what they were willing to do.

Jesus delivered the command, "Go." For the language enthusiasts out there, I am well aware that in its original Greek form, this is a verbal noun (participle), not a verb in the imperative (command) mood. I apologize for veering into rather technical "language speak," but it is important to note that, even though the English translation is clearly an imperative, the underlying language is not.

Some Bible scholars translate Jesus' words to "As you go" or "when you go" rather than simply, "Go." There is an argument for "Go" in that the participle can take on the characteristic of the verb it modifies—make disciples—which is in the imperative or command mood. So either way you want to translate it, "As you go" or "Go" can be defended.

But does it really make a difference whether Jesus commanded them to go or assumed that they would go? Within the context, the assumption of going seems even stronger than the command to go. Jesus couldn't conceive of His disciples *not* going! Especially since their training taught them to go; now the scope of going was enlarged.

Assumption of going seems even stronger than the command to go.

Perhaps He was making sure that they understood the nature of the mission. Before He had told them to only go to the Jews (Matt. 10:5–6) and to stay in homes where people had a spiritual interest (Matt. 10, Luke 10). This was part of their training and not their ultimate mission.

Jesus was crystal clear in His last command defining the mission of His followers. This final statement of Jesus outlines the bias to action, methodology, scope, and resources of those willing to take up His cause. Whatever happened to them until now was training for the rest of their lives.

I prefer to let the underlying language stand and see Jesus making an assumption that starts with, "As you go." My argument derives not only from the text itself but also the experience of the church.

The translation of "Go" has led us to develop a biblically foreign concept—evangelism—and a dichotomy foreign to Jesus' mindset—evangelism versus discipleship. This concept and dichotomy has crept into and diluted the power of Jesus' command. Since the Great Commission as Matthew delivers it doesn't have room for a proclaiming approach to advancing the faith, the translation taken as "Go" provides the crack in the door to read this concept back into this passage.

If we assume "going" to mean *evangelism* and "making disciples" as a companion to evangelism, we begin to see these commands as equally important. Adding a bifurcated process to Jesus' simple and direct command does injustice to the text and has had a lethal effect on the advancement of the good news.

The effect over the years is that followers of Christ build paradigms like "gather to disciple" and "scatter to spread the good news," both/and terminology, or the endless debate about being missional versus attractional. These pervading metaphors provide the battleground for Christians today to waste time on needless arguments. The evangelism/discipleship paradigm has colored how we read the Bible and corrupted our clear understanding of this pivotal passage.

DISCIPLE-MAKING DISCIPLES AREN'T THE NORM

No matter how you measure the practice of the church, multiplicative disciple-making (disciple-making that multiplies) has not been tried and found wanting; rather it has been tried, found difficult, and abandoned. There have always been voices at the edges begging for followers of Christ to capture the reproductive nature of Jesus' final command. But the main flow of energy and funds of modern Christianity have been put toward world evangelization rather than disciple-making. This is typified by the Lausanne movement that started as a conference on world evangelization. There has never been a conference or movement among global Christian leaders on world "discipling"!

The energies that have been piled into disciple-making have, for the most part, involved a knowledge-based approach. Since the Western world embraced Plato and his way of thinking, Western culture moved away from a Hebrew, unified worldview and developed a more patristic worldview. What flies under the term *discipleship* is foreign to Jesus' thinking. Our "discipling" is driven by the acquisition of knowledge.

Jesus never intended to split His mission or methodologies into evangelism and discipleship. Before you look up my address so you can tar and feather me for heresy, think through the Gospels. Where do you see Jesus engaging in anything like the evangelism we spend hours training people to do? It just doesn't exist.

When given the opportunity to break into what we would identify as a modern evangelism technique, Jesus did something very counterintuitive. In Mark 10, Jesus was asked by a spiritually interested person how to inherit eternal life. What an appropriate place for Jesus to bring out the Four Spiritual Laws, The Bridge to Life, or the Romans Road and walk this man right into the family of God. What a perfect place to model evangelism and how it ought to be done through the centuries. Jesus did what we would never do: He told the man to give away everything he had!

Continue on through the Gospels. Put aside your paradigm of persuasion evangelism. Did Jesus train His disciples to spread the good news this way? Did He model it for anyone? Why are we putting all of our energy toward persuasion evangelism to reach the unbelieving world when it is hard to find Jesus practicing it?

Just because the practice of persuasion evangelism is familiar and seems natural doesn't mean we shouldn't challenge it. History may be on my side; the invention of the altar call by Charles Finney (1792–1875) and the advent of the sinner's prayer began a move by Christ followers to synthesize legitimate biblical concepts into a formula for returning people to the family of God.

- If we confess with our mouth (Rom. 10:9–10)
- If we are faithful to confess our sins (1 John 1:9)
- Repent and be baptized (Mark 1:15)

There is nothing wrong with an altar call or the sinner's prayer, but there is nothing biblical about them either.[1] My goal in this discussion is not to extinguish any practice but to suggest that the Bible might be pointing us in a different direction, especially when we look at the results we are getting with our current methods.

The simplicity of a multiplicative discipling strategy has been robbed from Jesus' intended meaning by reading concepts into this passage that aren't there. Jesus gave a simple and compelling command, "Make disciples!" He assumed His followers would do nothing other than "Go."

He didn't intend for a special group of people called to take the message over the ocean to evolve from this command. He intended to embed this mission in the lives of everyone who follows Him. To be a follower of Christ is to be on mission. I think Jesus would find foreign the concept of a person becoming a Christian but not becoming a disciple until later when he or she becomes more committed to faith.

Jesus' hope was that it would be normal for His followers to make disciples as they lived out a dangerous message that would divide families and heal the brokenhearted, challenge the well-off and encourage the impoverished, transform the oppressors and bring freedom to the oppressed. To fail to make disciples would indicate followers weren't connected to Jesus and the heart of His mission (John 15:8).

DISCIPLES AS JESUS INTENDED

The prayer Jesus taught these disciples (Matt. 6) lays out the vision in a simple phrase "thy will be done on earth as it is in heaven." Jesus left heaven not to rescue humankind from earth but to get God out of heaven onto earth, to bring the rule of God. The Father and His Son as well as the Spirit dream of a transformed world—this world we live in, not just the one to come. They want to show off the power of the Creator to renew, restore, and rebuild the world they created and that humanity has destroyed.

How will this happen? Here is the command: Make disciples! Make learners, people who are ordering their lives around the Creator's wishes. To be abundantly clear, Jesus asks us to make disciples—not converts, not confirmands, not church members, not pastors, not clergy—but disciples.

And we are left asking again, HOW? Jesus gave two simple steps, first by baptizing and second by teaching obedience. It is important to note that these two phrases are coordinate. As you go, make disciples, baptizing them in the name of the Father, Son, and Spirit, and teach them to obey all things I have commanded. There is no distinction of time in one being placed first and the other second. Jesus could just as easily have turned them around, and it would not have made one iota of difference in the passage.

We often see His command interpreted in this way: first we evangelize, with success being defined by baptism; and then we teach or disciple. Jesus did not bring the bifurcation to the passage; we do. His methodology was one step—to disciple men and women into kingdom living. There are two significant and distinct yet equal processes that define making disciples:

- identifying them with a Jesus kind of life
- teaching them a life of obedience

IDENTIFY WITH A JESUS KIND OF LIFE

By substituting the word *identification* for *baptism*, I am not suggesting that we jettison the ancient rite of water baptism. I am suggesting that Jesus intended more than just a ritual that signifies washing away the debt of our rebellion against the Creator. Jesus commanded us to identify with Him.

Should the ritual of *baptism* make a statement to those with whom we live, learn, work, and play rather than just those in our spiritual communities? Have we settled for mindless ritualistic obedience rather than committing thoughtful energy to keeping the application of Jesus' command relevant in our world? Moreover, does this command call for a one-time event or does it suggest a lifelong process of helping people identify?

The Word exposes Jesus' assumption that His followers wouldn't be able to live the lives they once lived because they weren't the people they once were. Paul, a later follower of Jesus, took this into account when he began his letter to the Romans with a rhetorical question, "How should we respond to all of this? Is it good to persist in a life of sin so that grace may multiply even more" (6:1)?

Becoming a disciple starts a life-transforming process of repeatedly ordering our world, both inner and outer, around the thoughts and wishes of our Father in heaven. Baptism signifies the start of a life of learning how to be identified as living a "with-Jesus" life, a life that is spiritually obvious. Unfortunately modern Christianity has majored in teaching people to be spiritually obnoxious. We've taught people to share their faith rather than their lives. We've majored in teaching people to export propositions rather than to simply be open about their authentic experience with the living God.

Studies of the failure of modern churchgoers to share their faith litter the internet. Books, courses, seminars, and conferences abound on how we can get churches to be more evangelistic. Is the problem with the people? Do they just need a more radical faith? Or is the problem endemic in the system itself, and we simply need to stop trying to put new wine into old wineskins?

Baptism, the process of being identified with Jesus, is one half of the strategy that Jesus commissioned to move the message of hope and restoration to the ends of the earth. The second half of that strategy is equally powerful and significant—teach obedience to Jesus.

TEACH OBEDIENCE

I am always surprised when I ask groups of people to identify the main actions found in Matthew 28:16–20. Invariably "teach" is

Baptism signifies the start of a life of learning how to be identified as living a "with-Jesus" life.

separated from the phrase "to obey." We are about knowledge, not obedience.

Whatever the cause, removing "to obey" from "teach" shows gross negligence in reading the Bible. Jesus asked followers to teach people to obey all of His commands. What have we done in response? We've taught people all of Jesus' commands and assumed that knowing them means they will obey them. Many people—believers and nonbelievers—would give today's church a very low grade when it comes to obedience to Jesus' commands.

Why would we fail to see what is in plain sight: obedience? Do we assume that if you know something, you'll do it? We know we are supposed to eat healthy foods and that we should exercise, but does that mean we follow those rules on the whole? Our collective health report card would say no! Knowing and obeying are two very different things.

In reality, knowing doesn't lead to obeying. I learned that lesson as a parent. When I was disciplining my children, they would often say, "I know, I know." That exclamation was an attempt to defend their disobedience. So I developed this mantra for them: "Knowing means doing." Unfortunately *knowing, teaching,* and *learning* aren't necessarily connected with obedience.

Humans in general, and especially those raised in a political democracy, have an aversion to obedience. We are free, with con-stitutional rights. Phrases such as "You're not the boss of me." or "Who died and made you God?" can be heard throughout our land.

In weddings today, one of the discussions about vows will often be the bride wanting to make sure that "obey" is excised from the words to be recited. It just doesn't seem fitting for a human to obey another human in this modern era.

But what about the Creator? If He is the Creator and Designer of life as we know it, shouldn't He be consulted? Wouldn't He be the smartest, wisest, most competent being in the universe on living life? It just seems to make sense that if you believe in a Creator, then you would want His advice about how to live *in* and *as* His creation. So Jesus commanded us to adopt a methodology that teaches people to order their lives around God's wisdom.

In doing this, Jesus didn't fear the label of legalism, but boldly placed "teaching to obey all my commands" at the heart of His methodology. Modern Christianity, especially that which has been exported from the United States, is soaked in a perverted view of grace as tolerance and acceptance. The cultural cancer that has leaked into modern Christianity and that flies under these perverted concepts of grace has stolen the heart and soul out of Jesus' final command.

Legalism is holding people accountable to human laws. Jesus was not asking us to obey any rules or guidelines laid down by humans. Nothing could be further from the truth! The obedience Jesus commanded was not to Christian cultural standards or denominational practices. No, this obedience finds out what Jesus said (not a particular denomination or spiritual teacher) and considers Jesus' commands the standard by which to live. Obeying Jesus leads to freedom, not legalism.

Obeying Jesus leads to freedom, not legalism.

However we attempt to follow Jesus' command to make disciples, at the core of our activity is how we teach people to obey all of His commands. Our methodologies must carry out Jesus' intention to foster obedience-based cultures, cultures that learn to love God and others. These are not the extrabiblical rules of our denominations or churches but the commands found in the Bible. The goal is not to be deluded into thinking that knowing the commands is enough. We must exhibit them where we live, learn, work, and play. Being a true disciple is a matter of learning to obey what Jesus said.

How many discipleship programs do you know of in which teaching people to obey is the primary focus? I am sure we can all name many that teach people fundamentals of the faith, spiritual disciplines, leadership development, and ministry skills—but that is not what Jesus asked us to do. He commanded us to teach people to obey. How could we miss that?

It is not a secret that making disciples is a lost art in modern Christianity as Leroy Eims reminded us.[2] Dallas Willard's book *The Great Omission* is a stinging criticism of the modern church's failure to obey Jesus' last command.[3] As I write, thought leaders such as Alan Hirsch are sounding a warning signal that an authentic understanding of disciple-making has been all but extinguished in the modern church.[4]

A ONE-STEP PROCESS

Reading evangelism as Jesus' final command—turning a one-step process into a two-step process—tore the heart right from His strategy. Instead of figuring out how to disciple—teaching to identify with Jesus and to obey Him—we drifted toward converting people to a set of propositions and then attempting to get them to understand that Jesus wants to be more than their Savior.

We've taken a process of learning to make Jesus King and twisted it into a practice of using persuasion to get people to agree with a set of statements about themselves and God. The result is that we have organizations called churches full of consumers who assent to very important spiritual truths but don't live out the mission that Jesus set forth in Matthew 28:18–20. What we call church is nothing like Jesus intended.

There is nothing innately wrong with evangelism, altar calls, and the sinner's prayer but they aren't modeled, practiced, or commanded by the Bible. Nor do they deserve to provide the lens through which we read the Bible. If we can back out of that paradigm long enough to reread the Bible, we might see that there could be a different way.

An intimate gathering on a mountain provides the context for Jesus' commissioning of His followers. The final command was aimed at the group He had been with for three years. Everything He had done and said must be seen in the light of these words. This is not just His final command but His lasting commission to His followers. Matthew's version of the Great Commission is the most complete description of this commission and, therefore, deserves to define all of the other gospel writers' commissions rather than be defined by them.

So, to summarize, *baptism* focuses on the outward move toward Jesus, while *obeying* what Jesus said is the inward expression of a discipled life. The two come together as the world comes to see that we are coming to live a Jesus kind of life-obedience, as the Spirit leads us to exchange our addiction to self for affection to a new leader. The outward identification is a natural result of our will becoming submissive to our Creator who is the King and who is gradually and consistently becoming my King.

DISCIPLE-MAKING DISCIPLES

Let's jump back into the passage and pick up the extent to which Jesus suggested His disciples should envision reaching. The scope of this mission is quite clear. Earlier Jesus sent them to the Israelites. There is no question that now their disciple-making efforts are aimed globally—every nation.

This is not the first time they've heard these words from Jesus. In Matthew 24:14, Jesus, responding to these same disciples who asked a question about the end of the age, indicated that His message needs to be taken to the whole world and the good news exposed to every sociopolitical grouping in existence.

It might be easy to confuse the word *nations* with political boundaries, but this is not the underlying language. The word *nations* is plural and refers to all the heathen or non-Israelite peoples: every tribe, language, people, and nation. Hebrew ears would have heard this loud and clear without an ounce of doubt. He was asking them to extend their reach beyond Israel to every people group. The picture drawn in Revelation 5:9 and 7:9 is of this commission being fulfilled.

This is not a new thought. Abraham was chosen and blessed in Genesis 12 for the purpose of being a blessing to all the peoples of the earth. Jonah was sent outside of Israel to provide a warning and a way of escape for the Ninevites. God has always been on a mission to restore His creation to His family.

In the beginning of Jesus' commission, He established His position in the universe: unrestricted authority and power. As He ended, He also provided another unrestricted characteristic: His presence. Jesus planned to be personally involved in carrying out His dream to make disciples of all people groups. The beginning and end, unrestricted power and constant presence, gave the disciples a taste of the resources at their disposal. There was nowhere they could go, no circumstance they could face where they would be without Jesus' power and presence.

At the end of His stay on earth, Jesus drew His key followers together and gave them their marching orders. I am no language scholar, but here's my summary of what was said:

> I have been granted unrestricted power in all that exists, so as you go to all the people of the earth, show them how to become my apprentices where they live, learn, work, and play by starting to identify themselves with my community—my Father, myself, and the Spirit. Ignite in them a reproductive revolution through discovering how to live out all of the wisdom that I have left with you so that they will multiply themselves to the ends of the earth. I am going to be in this until it is done.

My encounter with this passage has been long and fierce. But seven years ago I suddenly read this passage in a totally different light. The insight that turned me on my head was rather simple but quite profound.

Let's start with a question: Does Jesus command us to make dis-ciples in Matthew 28:16–20? Before you answer, think for a moment: Is there any way that the answer to this question could be no? Could there be hidden in plain sight an understanding of these truths that is so simple yet profound beyond imagination?

My personal moment of revelation about this passage came when I was able to say, "No, Jesus is not asking me to make disci-ples." Early in my experience with Jesus, I was convinced that He wanted me to make disciples, that reproduction was normal for His followers.

The history of my life is littered with men and women in whom I've invested my time, people whose lives will never be the same because I stumbled into their paths and took risks because of my belief that I could make a difference. Once, a friend said to me, "I don't always like you, but my husband is a better man because of you." These are real people, with names and faces that I know personally. Not hun-dreds or thousands of faces in the crowd, but disciples in whose lives I immersed myself.

Jesus was calling me to make disciple-making disciples rather than simply to make disciples.

One day while reading this passage, the scales fell off and I had an epiphany that changed me deeply. As I looked at this passage, I realized that it meant the same thing to me as it meant to my disciples. *They* were to make disciples. Again, it may seem straight-forward, but I saw that Jesus was calling me to make disciple-making disciples rather than simply to make disciples.

The men and women that I discipled grew, they matured, they exposed their internal worlds, challenged their fleshly strategies, and learned to deny themselves and live with the cross at the center of their lives. They loosened their grip on their resources to allow more of their hard-earned cash to be available to God's work. They reached out to their coworkers and neighbors and invited them to church. They gave generously, served the poor and under-resourced, and they became better husbands and wives. What could be wrong with that?

Jesus didn't just call me to cause people to mature in their spiritual journeys. He called me to make disciple-making disciples. Replication is central to the last command of Jesus. He wanted me to have, in a spiritual sense, children and grand-children and great-grandchildren.

> [Jesus] called me to make disciple-making disciples.

My epiphany came as I realized that Matthew 28 spoke not just to what I was supposed to be doing but also to how I was supposed to be doing it—my methodology.

I love to read and delve deep into my internal world. I love books written by sages such as Brennan Manning, Teresa of Avila, Larry Crabb, C. S. Lewis, Henri Nouwen, G. K. Chesterton, and Dallas Willard to name a few. I love to gather people together and read these books, to ask ruthlessly honest and penetrating questions that gouge their souls. We are addicted to personal peace and comfort, so creating disequilibrium in people always promotes growth, and I love to be in the middle of it.

I made disciples out of my passion and giftedness. I was risky and challenging. I wasn't afraid to risk relational pain and friendship for the sake of spiritual growth. That was who I was, but it was not who many of my disciples were. They weren't hardwired the way I was. They couldn't disciple the way I disciple, because they weren't gifted and impassioned the same way I was.

There was a clash of personal significance and Jesus' commission. At first I threw a fit and asked, "Jesus, is this who you made me to be? This is what I am good at. Why would you take that away from me?" But as the personal storm subsided something happened.

I realized that it wasn't so much that I was good at making disciples but that I loved reading, challenging, poking, and prodding.

It gave me a great deal of satisfaction, but there was a hard truth: I could not reproduce that in many people. In the classic sports metaphor, I could play but I couldn't coach.

This realization changed the finish line for me. No longer could I measure success by making disciples. Now I had to ask a gut-wrenching question: Can my disciples make disciples? Was I working with them in ways they could use to work with others?

I started to realize that if I was going to be serious about the Great Commission, I was going to have to find a simple and repeatable methodology. I needed a methodology that would transcend giftedness, personality, and passion; I needed a way of making disciples that would model for them how to make disciples despite their spiritual resources.

Let's rejoin our trek through Matthew 28:16–20, beginning with my summary of what we were told:

> I have been granted unrestricted power in all that exists so as you go to all the people of the earth, show them how to become my apprentices where they live, learn, work, and play by starting to identify themselves with my community—my Father, myself, and the Spirit. Ignite in them a reproductive revolution through discovering how to live out all of the wisdom that I have left with you so that they will multiply themselves to the ends of the earth. I am going to be in this until it is done.

On this hilltop Jesus commissioned the first disciples. They were to be a reproductive force of obedient apprentices that reached into every people group that existed on the face of the earth. At the beginning of His commission, He declared that they would never meet a force stronger than Him. Now at the end He declares His intent to be there all the way through. All-powerful, all the time! No matter how long it takes, Jesus assures His disciples that when the end comes, He will be there.

PUTTING THE GREAT
BACK INTO THE GREAT COMMISSION

Matthew's passage is the most complete account we have of the mountaintop meeting. Others provide a brief insight into what could be considered a Great Commission (Luke 24:44–49; Acts 1:4–8; John 20:19–23), but all of them are understood in light of Matthew's account.

So back to the statement that began this discussion:

> The Great Commission subordinates every other command in the
> Bible so that all of Jesus' teaching should be understood in light of
> it and, therefore, it is the prime directive for the followers of Christ
> until His return.

The Great Commission is not just a command; it is a mission statement. It is Jesus' strategic plan to see the good news reach every generation in every geographical location on the earth. Notice that Jesus' plan was not to plant churches but to make disciple-making disciples.

Can you make disciple-making disciples who don't love God and others? NO! They wouldn't be a disciple of Jesus. If you have a discipleship program that doesn't result in people who are learning to obey Jesus in every area of their lives, you are doing Jesus an injustice by calling what you're doing "disciple-making." Maybe that is why we use the term *discipleship* instead. History has shown that we can do what we call discipleship without making disciples.

To be a disciple is to be growing in your obedience to *all* that Jesus commanded. Jesus' disciples began to display the same heart that He had toward the poor, the oppressed, orphans, widows, the over-indulgent—any of the issues and conditions we face on earth that aren't found in heaven. Disciples are here to transform this world's systems, not just its inhabitants.

When we introduce to the text of the Great Commission concepts that aren't in Jesus' intention, a systemic confusion results. The definition of a *disciple* in modern parlance is tilted toward knowledge rather than obedience. A two-step process of evangelism and discipleship becomes the working model for most of Christianity. Instead of making disciples, we make converts and call them Christians. Jesus asked us to make disciples who would bring heaven to earth.

This intrusion of thought in the Great Commission creates an argument between the Great Commission and the Great Commandments that is foreign to Jesus' thinking. They are seen as a both/and function of Christianity rather than in the cause/effect relationship that Jesus intended. The natural effect of disciple-making disciples is living out Jesus' commands, great and small and making more disciple-making disciples.

We seem to want to create new vocabulary to correct the misguided directions of the past, but doing so just entangles an already complex issue. Do we really need *missional* disciples? I think Jesus might look at us and say, "What?" A disciple who is apprenticed to Jesus is already *on mission*. Is there a need to add a modifier and create the perception that there are different classes of disciples?

> **A disciple who is apprenticed to Jesus is already *on mission*.**

Are we afraid to look at what is called the church and wonder out loud if it is truly connected to Jesus? Could the great tragedy of our day be that all of our evangelism efforts have made people twice as fit for hell? People have been taught to trust in a walk down the aisle or in praying a prayer rather than to obey what Jesus asked. As Scot McKnight argues in *King Jesus Gospel,* we've preached a gospel of forgiveness rather than a gospel of kingdom living.[5]

A proper view of the Great Commission is the foundation for understanding how we are to proceed into our world with the message of Jesus. By refusing to insert our modern-day evangelistic thinking into the text, we can gain fresh insight into what Jesus wanted us to do: make disciple-making disciples of every people group on the entire globe.

CORRECTING THE GREAT MISTAKE

STARTING TO TAKE
JESUS AT HIS WORD

At 11:00 a.m. on Sunday, Caucasians, African Americans, and Hispanic/Latinos, as well as many other ethnic groups are largely segregated in their own religious experiences. But that is just the beginning of the segregation. The Baptists, Catholics, Presbyterians, Methodists, Orthodox, Nazarenes, Church of Christ, Mennonites, Brethren, Pentecostals, and Charismatics can all be found in separate places. All are proud of their distinctions and separateness.

One can only imagine what Jesus would say about the situation. What was His intention? Was it naive multiculturalism? Certainly the picture that Revelation gives is just this (Rev. 5:9; 7:9). But is that possible in this sin-stained world? Countless church planters have sacrificed to make this happen and few have succeeded.

The religious racism that has survived the Civil Rights Act of 1964 is merely a symptom of a much deeper issue. We can treat symptoms, or we can attempt to find root causes. It doesn't take much of a medical mind to know that treating symptoms is a lifelong activity, whereas addressing root causes leads to a cure. One principle keeps us focused on root causes: form follows function.

On October 14, 1947, Chuck Yeager became the first human recorded to have flown faster than the speed of sound. No doubt his war record and bravery in this experimental program have earned him revered status in aviation history. But he stands on the shoulders of many men who lost their lives attempting to break the sound barrier.

The attempt to break the sound barrier caused a number of issues for aeronautical engineers. For example, propellers on traditional aircraft could not achieve the speed of sound without destroying the fuselage. Aeronautical engineers reasoned that the smoothest airflow over an aircraft would be achieved if the cross-section of the craft increased smoothly from front to back. This would be a problem once the wings started to protrude from the plane. The solution was to pinch the fuselage in at the wings: the result was the classic "Coke bottle" design of supersonic aircraft. Fortunately the designers adhered to a simple principle: form follows function. They were not so emotionally attached to the traditional power plant and propeller-driven design that they couldn't look toward a new jet engine and a new fuselage shape. They allowed *form*—the power plants and shape of the fuselage—to be submissive to *function*—flying faster than the speed of sound.

Their adherence to this principle not only allowed them to break the sound barrier but allowed for speeds in manned aircraft to exceed six and seven times the sound barrier. Our attention to simple principles can become both the ticket to and the hindrance of accomplishments beyond our imagination. Apply the universal principles, and they provide freedom to exceed; deny them and they are cruel task masters.

I have started two churches as the primary church planter, been a part of a launch team of another, and served for six years on the staff of an established church. Through this experience, I have observed several critical issues that lead to ineffectiveness in following Jesus' commission.

I have come to believe that those who long to see Jesus' mission accomplished in this world often fail to pay attention to the principle of "form follows function." We have put form before function.

Listen closely. There is a place for a collection of men and women who meet regularly to encourage and challenge one another to experience God where they live, learn, work, and play. But we've become worshipers of form and have not paid close attention to function.

How would Jesus comment on this? I think He might accuse us of "Ecclesialotry." Yes, we have become worshipers of form—church. Jesus might even ask, "Why are you doing what I said I would do—build my church—and not doing what I commanded you to do—make disciple-making disciples?"

Neither the biblical text nor the flow of biblical history supports the betrayal of Jesus' commission. Jesus made disciple-making disciples. The bulk of recorded biblical history finds Paul making disciples before churches formed and recognized leadership. Both Jesus and Paul practiced form following function. The biblical function of the mission, multiplicative disciple-making, provided the direction and the form of the churches that followed.

Both Jesus and Paul practiced form following function.

They seemed to know that if you make disciple-making disciples, the result is always a biblically functioning community—Jesus' church. But if you plant churches, you don't always get disciple-making disciples. Unfortunately, the history of the church exhibits buildings full of people who we would be hard-pressed to call disciples. By taking the liberty to put church development before disciple-making, we've polluted the mission Jesus set us on and crippled the very organism that He wanted to foster His global mission.

"Ecclesialotry" has all but gutted the biblical meaning of the word *church* in English. The infrequent use of the word in the Bible should have been a model for us. Yet our overuse and abuse has robbed us of the significance of *church*.

A brief side trip thru the etymology of *church* will help shed light on this discussion. The word *church* is probably derived from the Old English and German *kirche*, the Scottish "kirk" from which we derive our word *church*. It might be related to the Greek *kuriakos* meaning "pertaining to the Lord," which appears twice in the Bible—neither translated as church. You might ask at this point, "How does this relate to the term *ecclesia* which is usually translated "church" in the Bible?

Did our translators lead us astray by not simply translating *ecclesia* as "assembly"?

Did our translators lead us astray by not simply translating *ecclesia* as "assembly," which Robert Young does in Young's Literal Translation? The power of this word that has shaped our reading of the Bible cannot be understated. If centuries of readers read "assembly" rather than "church," would we have the perversion of the ecclesia today? Would we have misplaced the Missio Dei (mission of God)? Would there be such strong identity of the word *church* with a building? I am convinced that it would have been harder to redirect assembly to meaning bricks and mortar.

The Greek term for church, *ekklesia*, referred to a group called for a special purpose. Jesus' *ekklesia* was called to spread His message of hope and healing through a reconnection with the Creator God. It was never an end in and of itself. In the early church, when people were discipled into the family of God, they were surrounded by like-minded people. This group of people knew only one thing: teach people to identify with Jesus and to obey Him.

Since they knew only one thing, the majority of their activity focused on cultivating disciple-making disciples. Inherent in the disciple-making process was living out their new family relationship with the Creator, who was now their Father. Because they came to know Jesus through obedience, it was normal for them to love God and extend His love into their world. They would, in effect, be the answer to the prayer Jesus taught the disciples, "Bring about Your kingdom. / Manifest Your will on earth, / as it is manifest in heaven" (Matt. 6:10).

That hasn't always been the case. That word *church* has become synonymous with the building on the corner (or the church that meets in a house or missional community that meets on Thursday nights). That building or meeting has become known as a *place* for "church people"—a segment of culture largely defined by what they are against. While driving today, I saw a bumper sticker that summed up the cultural attitude toward the church, "I am for separation of Church and Hate!" Our church culture is so warped that George Hunter in *Church for the Unchurched* says that the church might be the biggest obstacle for people connecting with God.[1]

How could that be? The very institution designed to carry out the mission of Jesus on earth has now become the biggest obstacle to that mission. I know you might be like me. I am involved in a church that is hip, cool, and culturally relevant. We reach out to the poor and under-resourced, accept anyone (even gay couples), dress the way we want, engage in stopping the sex trafficking of children, provide jobs for the unemployed, and other redeeming activities. But it doesn't matter what we're doing today, because it doesn't change opinions developed from watching us in the past. We, the church, have been wrong on so many issues that erasing the history we are connected to is impossible.

People never get close enough to see how cool we really are. The church culture, fair or not, has earned a commonly held image that isn't going away anytime soon, and our neighbors and workmates see us as part of it. We don't start at neutral when we begin to approach our friends, neighbors, relatives, and workmates about our faith. We start somewhere in the negative.

Where did we go wrong? It would be nice to blame all this on Constantine and be done with it. He may be culpable in the corruption of Jesus' ministry, but he is far from alone. Many wrong turns have led us to this mess we are in, and all of them are tied to the principle of form following function.

CHURCH PLANTING VERSUS DISCIPLE-MAKING

I've already discussed the first mistake—church planting—to some extent. This may sound a little like I'm the pot calling the kettle black, since I have been a church planter, but my experience does give me an insider's point of view.

When we plant churches, what we really do is start church services. With few exceptions, the focus of building a core group, covering staffing functions, especially a worship leader, gathering critical mass, raising funds for a broad launch, finding an event center, and picking a launch date is all about establishing a regular weekly meeting.

The energy required to do this is enormous: recruiting and training key volunteers to lead small groups, children's ministry, youth ministry, set-up/tear-down teams, and financial teams to name a few. But unfortunately, that energy is all focused on building an organization, a bureaucracy in the best sense of the word. That bureaucracy is not a perpetual-motion machine that runs without any energy supply. On the contrary, it requires an enormous amount of energy; because it is new, most everyone in it has never done it before. No organization is self-sustaining. It takes energy input; unfortunately, the larger it grows, the more energy it takes.

No one would argue that the mission of a church plant is to sustain itself, but in reality, most of the energy expended until this plant reaches viability will be focused on keeping it alive. To keep the mission of Jesus in mind becomes a juggling act. Unfortunately, if I drop the Great Commission ball, my paycheck doesn't suffer. However, if I drop the church plant ball, my economic security is threatened.

Certainly, it is possible to do both; but in my experience the activity of church formation easily squeezes out the Great Commission activity.

The same could be true for missional communities, which are just a different form of church. To build a cohesive community among participants and get the vision shared and functioning takes energy; it doesn't happen on its own. Even though the critical issue is to get this group on mission, there is energy that goes into the dynamics of the group, energy that is communal rather than missional.[2]

It just isn't possible to build the kingdom of Jesus and plant a church or gather a missional community at the same time. Churches are planted today so that they can build the kingdom tomorrow. Missional communities are formed so that they can incarnate Jesus where they are. In order to achieve success, I must get the church system functioning or the missional community system functioning so that it can become a kingdom-building entity.

Many, if not all, church planters I know are genuinely interested in fulfilling the Great Commission. They believe wholeheartedly that church planting is the most effective tool to do this. So they faithfully put their shoulder to the plow and attempt to expand the kingdom of Jesus the best way they know how. But are they simply captives of a system that practices ecclesialotry? Somehow we have put the proverbial cart before the horse and can't find our way back to Jesus' true intention. Because it is easier to build form/plant churches, we do this instead of making disciple-making disciples. The truth is that we haven't figured out how to do multiplicative disciple-making! So we plant churches in hopes that disciples will appear. And then we inevitably act surprised when they don't.

The young men and women we encourage to plant churches are like the test pilots in the late 1940s who were dying at the rate of one per week. Our church planters are being asked to fly at supersonic speeds in aircrafts that are designed for subsonic travel. The point when they meet that barrier is rough and threatening. Some break through, but many don't.

Form follows function. Jesus commanded us to make disciples; that is our function. Paul traveled from city to city making disciples and, in the process, churches formed. Jesus was true to His word, and Paul was true to the function Jesus commanded.

"If we want Jesus-sized results, we are going to have to use Jesus' method," as my friend and international trainer Jim Yost is fond of saying. What he means is a return to letting Jesus build His church and a shift in focus toward what He commanded us to do—make disciple-making disciples.

DEFINITIONS ARE IMPORTANT

We may all agree we have a problem. But what is the way back?

Words and how we use them make a difference in how we think and act. We see that in our own personal lives. We tell a story about someone and use a descriptor for skin color or nationality inadvertently, when if the person's skin color or nationality was the same as ours, we wouldn't have added the descriptor. Why? Because it betrays an insidious and often hidden racial attitude we haven't confronted. Words and how we use them are reflective of our deeper reality.

Using words created for beautiful purposes in immoral ways is etymological pornography. Changing the intended meaning by over-using words and phrases until they no longer have any connection to their original intention is immoral. The word *immoral* may seem stringent, but how long are we going to pretend that calling buildings "churches" hasn't corrupted modern Christianity? The term *church* or *ekklesia* does not refer to bricks and mortar, yet we've acquiesced to this in Western culture and then re-exported it to the world.

Recently, while traveling in Kenya, a friend said to me, "You gave us the virus, now you must bring the anti-virus." He was referring to the African churches' addiction to titles and fixation on a Western style of building centric ministry.

First, using the term *church* to refer to a building gives people the idea that there is a "First Church" that is above, beyond, or apart from them. I remember when serving on the staff of a church, an elderly lady called and said, "When is the church going to do something about Kathryn Baker's birthday?" I responded, "I don't know, when are you?" That response, in addition to other reasons, is why I am no longer employed by that church!

What if we placed the phrase "meets here" on all of our church signage and began to move toward consistency in using the term *church* only for the people. This has been a lifelong crusade for me, so when Shoal Creek acquired a building, I refused to let my family call it a "church." I even fought a losing battle with our leadership team to keep "Community Church" off our building sign. They felt that despite the theological error, it was necessary from a cultural standpoint. It was decided that people have a hard enough time going to a church meeting in a building. Making them guess what we were would make it harder for them to attend. I lost that battle! It is a simple thing, and may seem insignificant, but it is a fight that makes a point. It is driven by the idea that the church is a movement of people, not an organization that lives in a box on the corner.

Second, because we've just discussed church as people not buildings, let's be clear what we mean when we use the word *church*. I am often perplexed as to why we can accept the use of the term *church* for Arab brothers and sisters who meet secretly as a family in their home in Riyadh, Saudi Arabia, but when someone calls what looks like a small group a "church" in North America, we get all bent out of shape.

The church is a movement of people, not an organization that lives in a box on the corner.

Let's at least have enough biblical integrity to have our own defi-nition of *church*. Would this describe what we mean when we use the word *church*?

- A religious institution made up of paid professional (clergy) and laity

- A paid professional (clergy) who will lead the work

- Passive laity who pay the clergy to do the most important work

- Constitutions and by-laws

- A building

- Registered nonprofit status with the government

- A set of doctrines that defines it as different from other local churches[3]

Even though everything in us wants to shout, "NO!" to each of these, we have a little problem. The famed organizational psy-chologist Chris Argyris points out our problem in his book *Theory in Practice*. In effect, Argyris suggests that we are all liars. We espouse one theory and yet practice another. Unfortunately, people act on the basis of their mental models, which are driven by the theory in practice. What they say is more of a wish or hope of what might or could be.[4] This is not a religious, spiritual, or church problem, it is a human problem and can be found in most organization created by humans. We declare that the church is the people; yet again and again, we are involved in conversations where a building is referred to as "the church." We speak out of both sides of our mouths. We say one thing and do another.

While working with friends in Europe, I was really surprised at the energy and pride they exhibited when they received notification from the government that they were an official church.

Notwithstanding the cultural issues, I argued that they won a battle but ultimately will lose the war. If we are going to plant churches to reach this area, and every church plant in the area has to expend that kind of energy and wait for the government to give them a certificate to be declared a legitimate church, the rapid expansion of the good news throughout the area is doomed. Their structures are much too heavy to move through swiftly. They are working and thinking on the wrong plane.

This type of thinking relies on a fleshly, material type of wisdom that assumes people will see you differently if an earthly entity provides credibility. It shows a reliance on the material world and a lack of trust in the Spirit to move in, enlighten, and regenerate. The return on investment is small and short-term. The return on investment in making disciple-making disciples lasts a lifetime. The disciple-making investment may take longer to pay off; but when it does, it pays in much higher dividends.

My mentors in the Disciple-Making Movements strategy are often accosted when they share what God is up to around the world.[5] In just one of the more than one hundred movements in the last twenty years, more than two million people have been baptized, and eighty thousand churches have been planted.[6] Immediately upon hearing those numbers, the question erupts, "How do you define church?"

Most of us can't conceive of churches multiplying that rapidly, so there must be something wrong with the definition of church. You can't build eighty thousand church buildings in that short a time, much less fund them! I think we are so plagued by our etymological pornography and our violation of the form/function principle that we can't see our own issues. We are much like fish that never feel wet. Wet is a fish's natural state. Wet is normal; it is the baseline for everything about being a fish. For a fish to become aware of its wetness, it is going to have to experience dryness. Now this experience of discovery will bring risk, fear, danger, disequilibrium, and discomfort to its life. The fish will grow in its awareness and appreciate wetness so much more, but it has to experience the discomfort of dryness to do so.

This book is about that kind of discomfort for me. Growing through the paradigm shifts helped me become aware of my "wetness" and begin to examine whether it was biblical, cultural, historical, amoral, or immoral.

Even though I have a theological degree from one of the most academically rigorous graduate schools of theology, I had to go back to some basics. I had to revisit definitions, how I used words. Could I define even the simplest of words: *church*?

How do you define church? If you saw one, how would you recognize that you found one? What are the minimal requirements for this entity to exist? What did Jesus command us about the church? What do we find in the rest of the Bible about church? Is there a difference between what is commanded and what is described? I am not going to attempt to answer all of these but I will take a shot at some.

It would be best for everyone to do their own work on this subject. It is so easy to read someone else's words and accept them. The problem is that we aren't committed to or convinced of anything other than our own conclusions. But I suppose since you spent money on this book that you deserve to hear mine.

Remember, we are starting at the lowest common denominator. What are the minimal requirements to have a church?

A church is a group of people who

- relate to God through obedience to His wisdom in the Bible
- relate to one another through regular connections for mutual encouragement and challenges
- relate to their world by bringing God's order from heaven to earth through multiplicative disciple-making.

The Bible is not bashful about the use of the term *church/ecclesia* for a group of people early in the development. Paul returned from Arabia to Jerusalem, then went off to Syria and Cilicia. As he described his travels that took place in AD 33–34, he mentioned that he wasn't known to the churches in Judea (Acts 9:31).

Barely three or four years after Jesus' death and resurrection, multiple churches existed in the Judaean region, long before Paul wrote to Timothy about the qualifications of leaders in a church. Is it fair to assume that these were minimalist churches? These groups of disciples who returned from Jerusalem after Pentecost began biblically functioning communities that Paul referred to as churches.

> **We haven't had the patience or principle to let form (planting churches) follow function (making disciples).**

No organism starts fully formed. There is a developmental process that is driven by the DNA encased in its primal cellular structure. If it grows too quickly, there are a set of issues that it faces; if it grows too slowly, there are another set of issues it faces.

Churches are no different. Unfortunately, the DNA of obedience-focused disciple-making (not to be confused with the knowledge-based approaches often described as discipleship) has rarely been in the primal cells of most churches. We have focused so much on the external pieces of modern church with our church-planting strategies that we haven't had the patience or principle to let form (planting churches) follow function (making disciples).

One problem in North America is that we are not minimalist but maximalist. When we plant a church, we focus on building systems in areas such as leadership, finance, membership, groups, outreach, marketing, music, and volunteer recruitment. It is as if we are going to assemble the skeleton before we have the cellular DNA in place.

Jesus and Paul didn't do this. Why do we do it? God may have created the world out of nothing, but churches can't and shouldn't be created that way. The right ingredients need to be in place to get the kind of church Jesus envisioned: a core group of men and women who are growing in their desire to obey Jesus and inviting those where they live, learn, work, and play to join them. Having a multiplicative disciple-making strategy in place should be the first priority in our church-planting strategy.

God may have created the world out of nothing, but churches can't and shouldn't be created that way.

What if the norm for church planting was at least three to four generations of disciple-making disciples before any regular public meetings were scheduled? The standard of establishing multiplicative disciple-making first and foremost would bring DNA to a church plant that could revolutionize the spread of Jesus' good news.

Jesus was on a mountain with a mixed group of worshipers and doubters through whom He was going to plant churches. None of us would be filled with unspeakable joy if these guys were our church-plant team. Yet Jesus went ahead and issued His Great Commission. He trusted that this was an organic process guided by the Spirit. He began building His church and, despite our efforts to muck it up, it has survived and spread around the globe.

Paul likewise went about connecting with people and nurturing their spiritual journeys. He wasn't always in one place for long, but the power of the good news took hold in people's lives when they were discipled into the family of God.

Paul's journeys took place over a period of thirteen years, nine of those years traveling. He may have visited as many as forty-eight cities. There was not enough time or energy for Paul to do what we do in church planting. He chose to put the DNA of obedience-focused disciple-making in place and allow the Spirit to work.

What we see is Paul making disciples in every place he went. He lays down a gospel DNA in people so that the organic nature of the church could be grown by Jesus. Paul didn't have a church-planting mentality; he had a disciple-making mentality. He knew that form (church development) must follow function (making disciples).

As this DNA grows and develops, we see Paul wrestling with timely issues, identifying those maturing in their faith to bring appropriate form to the function that developed. The structures were lightweight, function-driven, and led from behind rather than out front.

SIMPLE STRUCTURE IS REPEATABLE

The simplicity of lightweight structure promotes the organism's mission better than heavy and complex structure. A good test for any organization is the removal of the leaders. Will the organization carry on? Does it have a chance to survive? If not, the leadership was heavy and repressive, failing to build systems or structure that has the replicating genius of the Great Commission.

Every healthy organism moves from simplicity to complexity in a chaordic fashion. Complexity doesn't necessarily overburden the organism, just as the Bible didn't overburden the church with structure. We are not told when to meet, what is supposed to happen when we meet, how big or how small we should be; nor are we given any other particulars, except the kind of character our key influencers should have.

But that hasn't stopped us from developing Books of Order, Confessions, Creeds, Articles of Religion, Rules of Order, Papal Canons, and Manuals of Disciples that fill in the details that God saw fit to leave out. Everyone adds complexity. That is just a mathematical reality. It takes discipline to see the complexity you add and evaluate whether you are contributing to heaviness or improving functionality.

Let's revisit my definition of a church using simpler terms. The church is a group of people who

- obey God
- live exhibiting their obedience in community with like-minded disciples
- seek to change their world by discipling the world into the family of God

It is simple, I will grant you that. Remember, we need a functionally biblical definition of minimal requirements for the church. When it first emerges, it may be only a handful of people. As it multiplies through a neighborhood or workplace, it may grow and divide like a cell does. It will gain specificity as it needs to and will continue to organize itself along the key embedded values—make disciple-making disciples who identify with and obey all of Jesus' teachings.

Language is essential to building this growing culture. Every person who works cross-culturally in either business or mission knows that until you learn the language, you won't be able to understand the culture. When attempting to take the good news of Jesus to a city or region to create a movement, language is critical.

I believe that is precisely why Paul wasn't rigid on titles. In 1 Timothy 3:1 he referred to bishops, and in Titus 1:5 he referred to elders. He was describing the character of those who aren't appointed leaders but are recognized for what is already being produced by the Spirit in them. Their position of influence comes via character. What they are called is not the point; the function they serve is strategic.

The *Saturday Night Live* 40th anniversary show presented an example of this type of leadership. Although *Saturday Night Live* is not always a positive influence in our world, it has survived the test of time. But the anniversary show was not built around Loren Michaels, its founder and executive producer. Yes, he was mentioned

When attempting to take the good news of Jesus to a city or region to create a movement, language is critical.

numerous times but never appeared on stage until the finale. Forty years of celebration revolved around the people who made the show, not its founder, executive producer, and current leader.

It is clear from Jesus' teaching that titles were a detriment to the type of leadership He wanted. The function they serve is far more important. Jesus wanted leadership that leads from behind, the quiet powerful influence of men and women who are catalysts. They live to grow things beyond them. It is not about being in the middle or at the front, but letting the power of the gospel move beyond them. Their personalities, passions, and giftedness are not front and center. They have discovered how powerful the kingdom of Jesus can be when they practice the leadership style Jesus taught.

In Matthew 23:6–12, Jesus forbids the use of the title Rabbi, father, or teacher.

> They love the place of honor at banquets and the best seats in the synagogues and elaborate greetings in the marketplaces, and to have people call them 'Rabbi.' But you are not to be called 'Rabbi,' for you have one Teacher and you are all brothers. And call no one your 'father' on earth, for you have one Father, who is in heaven. Nor are you to be called 'teacher,' for you have one Teacher, the Christ. The greatest among you will be your servant. And whoever exalts himself will be humbled, and whoever humbles himself will be exalted. (NET)

The first reason for not using those terms relates to God fulfilling those roles in our lives. The second is tied to the "behind" role that Jesus intends for the key influencers in the kingdom.

Is it too much to infer from this command that titles, when they imply religious superiority, are not in Jesus' plan? What does that say about our use of the title *pastor*? I would submit that once again we've veered into etymological pornography with this word related to shepherding.

What a beautiful concept shepherding is. The function is absolutely necessary in any movement of God. But we've trashed the beauty by taking a gift (Eph. 4:11) and making it a title. Wouldn't "call no man teacher" in Matthew 23:10 include calling someone pastor? The word for *teacher* in Matthew 23:10 and *teacher* in Ephesians 4:11 are the same word. Take a look at the passage for yourself.

> It was the *risen* One who handed down *to us such gifted leaders*—some emissaries, some prophets, some evangelists, as well as some pastor-teachers—so that God's people would be *thoroughly* equipped to minister and build up the body of the Anointed One.

Read those words not as titles but as functions. I applaud efforts to reestablish the fivefold functions in the church: Apostles, Prophets, Evangelists, Pastors, and Teachers. It is a worthy task to focus on the functions that Jesus gave His church, but when it veers into establishing new titles and offices, it violates Jesus' leadership teaching.

Jesus and Paul never intended people be placed in socioreligious stations.

I realize that I am arguing against thousands of years of church history, but if language creates culture, then by our language we've created a spiritual hierarchy that erodes the very nature of every person called to make disciple-making disciples. By the mere use of terms denoting spiritual hierarchy, we've violated Jesus' clear command. Is it a stretch to see the command of Jesus in Matthew 23 controlling any and all titles we might use in the church to change the world? I don't think it is a stretch at all. In fact a violation of this command has created the "clergification" of the church.

Just like the caste system in India, which fixes people into socioeconomic stations in society, use of the terms *pastor, elder, deacon*, and any other labels we've come up with stratifies the church and builds dependency that Jesus never intended. Jesus and Paul never intended people be placed in socioreligious stations. Paul carried Jesus' leadership spirit forward by describing what these leaders do.

POST-REFORMATION MINISTRY

If I were to ask, "Are we doing post-Reformation ministry?" you might answer, "Well of course, on a timeline we are post-Reformation. Not a hard question to answer!"

When you look at how people connect with God in the pre-Reformation and post-Reformation periods, nothing has changed. Whether you are in a seeker church, attractional ministry, or missional community, we still ask those disconnected to God to connect with an individual or an institution before they can expect to connect to God.

Whether it is incarnational ministry, attractional meetings, or friendship evangelism, we still practice gospel outreach by connecting people to person or a place in an effort then to connect them with God. We use terminology such as "earn the right to be heard" or "build bridges before you cross them" or "be credible in a relationship"—all in an attempt to connect to an individual before connecting them to God.

Protestants accuse Catholics of heresy because they see the Virgin Mary, the clergy-led Mass, confession and the sacraments as humans mediating grace. Yet the Protestant orthopraxy of connecting people to people before connecting them to God is also mediation.

It is hard for us to conceive of connecting people to God without an intermediary. But theologically that is exactly what we believe. There is one God and one mediator (I Tim. 2:5), but somehow we feel the need to mediate the message to the uninitiated before Jesus can do His mediating work.

Learning to use the discovery process to take spiritually interested people to a relationship with God allows us to put our energy into connecting people with God rather than with ourselves. Their first dependency in their spiritual lives is on God and not on us.

RESURRECTION OR GIVING BIRTH?

Sometimes I am asked whether it would be more effective to help existing churches change or just go start something new. The adage, "It is easier to give birth than perform resurrections" is usually tossed about in this conversation.

Without worrying about sounding politically correct or trying to play both sides against the middle, I will say that neither approach is more effective. The simple truth is that both start at the wrong point. Both are stuck on creating form rather than building function. Both are going to engage in bureaucracy building. More energy is going into the form than the function.

Take, for instance, the existing church. A leader gets a whiff of this thing called a Disciple-Making Movement and wants to talk his fellow leaders into going over the cliff with him. There is a meeting of the church leadership, lots of discussion about something most of them don't even understand. The conclusion is that Disciple-Making Movements really are not biblical or are too radical, and so the decision is no go.

The leader with the vision goes away wounded and spends half the night railing to his spouse or close friends about how little commitment his fellow leaders have to the Great Commission. It takes days, if not weeks, to get back to some sense of normal. Thoughts of resignation swirl, but working at Starbucks doesn't sound all that appealing, and so he stuffs it in an emotional closest and begins to stumble forward.

Are his fellow leaders really less committed to the Great Commission? I am not sure this meeting reveals that. You see, the leaders in that room bought a ticket on a train headed to a destination. There was a vision, even if it was unclear or not shared. That vision represented the destination for the train they knew they were committed to riding. When our visionary showed up to share what God is up to around the world and how, if we could just open our eyes, we could see amazing things happen in our area as well, in effect, he was suggesting that the destination of the train be changed.

Let's face it, if you bought a ticket and got on a real train going to one place and suddenly the conductor announces, "Yes, we were headed in that direction, but we are about to shift to a new direction," you'd be pretty ticked off.

There is a basic issue of respect here. If you want the train to go in a different direction, you are going to need to get a lot of people who have already bought into moving in one direction to agree to go in another. That doesn't work well with people, especially not with church people. Church people feel that their direction is holy, ordained by God, and you better have some stone tablets with you if you are going to change the destination of this train!

So yes, resurrection is difficult! Despite the joy of real resurrection, there is a lot of relational turmoil to move through before the celebration. Perhaps the physical match of birth and resurrection plays well in speaking, but a better comparison might be giving birth and remodeling an old house. Why? Because everyone knows that it usually takes twice as long and costs twice as much as you planned to remodel something.

Remodeling can be dangerous to your health. I live in a house that is over one hundred years old. I know from experience that when you begin to remove the plaster you don't always know what you'll find. Your best efforts to learn, probe, and seek advice can't keep you from harm. Once, while removing a wall with a reciprocal saw, I felt a strange sensation. I joked, "maybe I'll find a dead body," only to discover I had just hit a gas line that I didn't know about. The next spark could have produced a dead body—me!

Too many desperate church leaders have gone off to the suburbs of Chicago, Los Angeles, Seattle, Atlanta, or Charleston and returned with what they thought was the most exciting and innovative direction for their churches, only to discover that few, if any, shared their enthusiasm for the new destination. Then the cycle of despair begins. Whether you call it "resurrection" or "remodeling," it is difficult at all levels.

Resurrection may be painful, but giving birth is expensive! In *Planting Fast Growing Churches* Stephen Gray, a veteran church planter, comes clean:

> Let's not be shy about it: church planting is very expensive. If you are not willing to invest multiple thousands in a church plant, don't even begin. Remember the old adage, "You get what you pay for"? Whoever coined that phrase must have been a church planter. If you are a denominational leader and you want to start a new church by rubbing a couple of dimes together, remember, "You get what you pay for." The quickest way to kill a church plant or at least doom it to a life of anemic survival, is to shortchange it. [7]

He goes on to put a dollar figure to this thought at somewhere around $200–300 thousand within a two-year period. This is chump change for those who traffic in illegal firearms or for your local drug czar, but for starting a church, even within a denomination, that is quite a tough sell. At a minimum of $150 thousand a year for three years, we are beginning to talk some serious money.

When you begin to do the numbers, it gets crazy. The Global Church Planting Network says that we need between twenty thousand and one hundred thousand new churches in the United States to see the Great Commission fulfilled.[8] At a yearly start-up cost of $150 thousand, we're looking at an extra $3 billion a year from Christians to approach fulfillment of the Great Commission. Does anybody think that is going to happen? Not I! Statistics show that the American church is less generous now, after a half-century of unprecedented prosperity, than it was at the depth of the Great Depression.[9]

The American church is less generous now . . . than it was at the depth of the Great Depression.

John Dickerson, after studying the giving trends of the modern church in the United States, says, "Unless giving trends change significantly, evangelical giving across the board may drop by 70 percent during the next twenty-five to thirty years. A recovery of the United States economy will not have a bearing on dropping ministry income—unless generational patterns change drastically."[10]

If planting churches is the most effective means of achieving the Great Commission, I am fully convinced that we are a long way from seeing the gospel get to every nation. Worldwide, eight out of every ten non-Christians don't even know a Christian.[11] How are we going to use our current methods to bridge that gap? The enormous funds required by our current forms make the task impossible. It requires a different way of thinking about moving the good news into these areas. Our form-fixed methods are in the way of the hope that we possess.

We don't have to give up on the idea of a biblically functioning community; we just need to reorder our understanding of the last command of Jesus. Our job is to make disciple-making disciples by embedding the biblical DNA of obedience and reproduction into them. Jesus will build His church from His obedient followers. We can repent of our ecclesialotry and get back to Jesus' intended mission.

FROM MINISTRY TO MOVEMENT

MIND SHIFTS NECESSARY TO SET THE GOOD NEWS FREE

hifts in thinking come in two ways: rapid and radical. The difference between the two is one of substance, not of degree. I led a two-day team-building conference for a company in the southeast United States that sold supplies to the printing industry. Their business had experienced *rapid* shifts for about fifty years. For example, technology was making it less expensive and more reliable to print four-color processes in shorter runs.

But in the early 1990s, radical shifts began to take place. The digital world introduced them to a different reality. Now they were losing 30 percent of their products every year and facing extinction as a company. It was time for their leadership team to think differently about the future.

When radical shifts occur, depending on old ways of thinking can be lethal. It is not possible to do what we used to do better; we have to do it differently. The problem arises because our surroundings in these times are not that different. There are many things that look and act the same, but the underlying principles are very different. It is as if you were playing in a baseball game, closed your eyes, and woke up in a cricket game. There is a ball, bat, and base, but everything else is radically different.

A friend once plopped down in my office, frustrated that he had just wasted an hour. The smile on his face betrayed that there was a story to be told. So I asked, "What's up?" He obliged with a tragic mental shift that failed to happen.

He needed to contact MasterCard, so he called the operator, who told him to dial 1–800–MASTERCARD. Being an analytic, he looked at that and thought, "That's too many letters to represent a phone number."

You can see his paradigm; phone numbers have ten digits. There were too many letters in M-A-S-T-E-R-C-A-R-D to represent the last seven digits he needed to call his credit card company. Since the information he was given didn't fit his paradigm, he began to problem solve.

On a legal pad, he began to write down all the iterations of M-A-S-T-E-R-C-A-R-D that fit into his paradigm. He dialed each one, being careful to record his experimentation. Take out the vowels, abbreviate in a logical fashion, and so on. It wasn't long before he had a legal pad full of all types of alphabetic variations.

All this activity ended in frustration, as none of the numbers worked, so he redialed information and asked again for the number, fearing operator error on the other end in the first conversation. He got the exact same answer so he commented to the voice on the other end, "Isn't that too many numbers?" And before the voice could answer, he went into an impressive review of his experiments with the derivations.

The voice let him finish, then asked a question that pierced deeply, "Did you try 1–800–MASTERCARD?" Embarrassed to answer, my friend quickly ended the call.

With fear and trepidation he dialed 1–800–MASTERCARD. Lo and behold, he got the connection he was looking for. An hour of his life lost in his own mental patterns; an hour of eternity gone due to paradigm paralysis.

Hardening of the categories causes us to miss great opportunities. Joe Green, Mark Zuckerberg's college roommate, turned down the chance to partner on Facebook based on his father's advice.[1] The difference between yes and no was about $7 billion!

We are not dealing with money, though, but something far more valuable—men and women made in the image of God. It is imperative that we challenge our mental patterns, our paradigms, so that we see the truth that God has communicated in ways that He intended.

FROM KNOWLEDGE TO OBEDIENCE

I want to take a look at three areas where our patterns of thinking are restricting the free flow of the good news of Jesus' life, death, and resurrection. The first of those areas is a shift in thinking from knowledge to obedience. As discussed earlier, when reading Matthew 28:16–20, it is not uncommon for people to cruise right past the word *obedience*, simply understanding it as, "teach all things that I have commanded."

The problem is larger than just this passage. As the gospel traveled west from Palestine, a subtle yet lethal misunderstanding crept into the practice of the church. This aberration can be traced to the good news having been born in a Hebrew culture and moving rapidly into predominantly Greek-influenced cultures.

The Hebrew mental framework was a unified view of existence. The source of that unity was found in the Creator of the universe who was infinite, or unlimited in any and all of His attributes. Therefore all of His communications and actions were consistent simply because they were His. The Creator's communications might seem contradictory from a human view, but the Hebrews embraced their own finiteness; they were okay with the fact that they were limited in capacity. They were comfortable with never being able to make sense of things since they would never approach the unlimited knowledge of the Creator.

For instance, the Bible communicates that God has ordained all things (Rom. 8:28; 11:36). It also teaches that prayer changes things (Matt. 7:7; James 4:2). For a Hebrew, these two ideas may stimulate questions and catalyze much discussion, but both are held in tension. The desire to make them make sense would never violate the truth of either, no matter how frustrating it might be.

The Hebrews never assumed that they could come to final resolution of the Infinite's seemingly contradictory statements or actions. This presumption of a limited perspective allowed them to accept apparent contradictions. They were able to live with the tensions in their understanding of the divine because they accepted their finite point of view, albeit uncomfortable.

This unified view also leached into their behavior. They couldn't conceive of knowing and doing being separate. To know something was to act on it. God was not someone to be primarily understood but one to be obeyed.

The Greek framework was built on a particular view of existence espoused by philosophers like Plato. He divided the world of the physical and the metaphysical. The metaphysical was the world beyond what you can touch and see and feel. Often thought of as the mental or spiritual world, this world in Plato's estimation was the best of the worlds. The realm of ideas and concepts was the ultimate reality. Truth is obtained through the intellectual exercise of philosophy by which additional ideas and concepts are discovered. "In this way, the world of our existence is dualistic. The material world has no essential meaning in and of itself. Only the form or idea gives meaning. If a person is to have true knowledge, then, he must find it in His mind, not in the world in which he lives."[2]

The followers of Jesus expanded out of Palestine into cultures influenced by the Greek dualism found in Plato, and we see the effects in even the earliest churches. The church in Jerusalem struggled with the practice of Jewish laws among non-Jews (Acts 15), and in Corinth they had a problem with living out the sexual values Jesus desired (1 Cor. 5). Each of these was a clash of the spiritual world with the material world.

There are two basic assumptions issuing from Plato that create difficulty engaging the biblical truth. The first is the separation of the material and immaterial worlds. There is no harm in looking at that division as an observation of reality. The harm comes in elevating one over the other. From the Hebrew unified world, the two were causally linked; but in the Greek, the immaterial was most important.

The second assumption challenges human finiteness. The assumption is that the immaterial has all the answers to life, and these answers are discoverable. Again, there is nothing harmful in that by itself; but in the Greek mind, it was possible to find the "unifying" principle of the universe. In other words, it was possible to understand God. It is possible to understand things about God, but for the finite to completely understand the infinite is an eternal impossibility.

As this has played out in modern days, we see that the definition of discipleship has, for the most part, become an acquisition of knowledge, hoping that it will then spur holy action in the physical world. The problem resides in our lack of understanding of our own presumptions. In the same vein as a fish not feeling wet because wet is its normal environment,[3] we don't feel the influence of Plato's dualism because it is so deeply embedded in our Western culture.

With an affection for the world of ideas, modern Christians pursue "knowing" over "doing." I know that is a broad characterization, but the point is proved by the moral statistics we have already examined and by simply looking at the way we "do" church.

With an affection for the world of ideas, modern Christians pursue "knowing" over "doing."

A gifted communicator who has digested biblical truth stands and delivers this truth to the faithful. He (as often is the case) displays his grasp of the Bible in front of large numbers of people. He is hopeful that something will stick and lives will change. Never is someone asked upon returning the next Sunday, "What did you do with what you learned last week?" There is a clear desire to learn more rather than to obey more.

This dualistic default mode, which modern Christianity operates under, builds an addiction mentality for knowledge. Since the knowledge is a false attempt at satisfying something that can't be satisfied, the law of diminishing returns applies and sets up the addiction cycle. The last hit of knowledge didn't satisfy, so I need more. I need and seek relief of my eternal itch. That relief comes in the form of new information about God, Jesus, and the Bible. That information satisfies momentarily but wears off eventually. I seek more information, but the previous doses aren't sufficient, I need more than before. The cycle continues because I have this unseen yet undeniable thought that I can understand God or, as the Greeks would say, "find the unifying principle of the universe." When I do I'll find what I've been looking for.

This Greek way of thinking seduces us into assuming that more is better. This is directly related to the addiction issues, but is slightly different in nature. If a little is good, more is better. So we value people who can write and speak well. If I am going to obey something, however, I might want less information to work with rather than more. If information is going to help me obey, it's because information helps to explore the truth in smaller portions.

We get this in theory when it comes to calories. Hitting the buffet restaurant several times a week challenges a person's girth. Unless there is adequate exercise commensurate with the calorie intake, dangerous health issues can arise. The same is true when we ingest large amounts of truth without appropriate acts of obedience.

The Pharisees represented a culture that "knew" a lot of spiritual truth. The presence of so much truth without obedience creates a superiority, a self-righteousness and an inability to hear the truth itself. The same might be true of modern Christianity!

The God of the Bible is meant to be related to and obeyed. We can understand things about God, but we are finite beings with limits to our understanding. Being controlled by a deep-seated demand to completely grasp the infinite is to deny the created order. When this demand quietly drives our discipleship programs, a perverted system develops. As a result we fail to heed Paul's warning in Romans 12:2, "Do not be conformed to this world." It is not just the acts of disobedience in the world he is addressing but also the systems of thinking that inform the ways of the world.

It was no mistake that God entered the world as a Hebrew. Pouring eternal truth through a human culture that lived out the created synergy between the material and immaterial was divinely designed. Conversely, the failure of modern Christianity to understand our platonic way of separating the material and spiritual is the Achilles heel to the spreading of the good news.

FROM ANALYSIS TO SYNTHESIS

This great big fat Greek way of thinking has led us to favor analysis rather than synthesis in our handling of the Bible. In certain corridors, verse-by-verse teaching is lifted up as the gold standard of biblical oration, inductive Bible study touted as superior, and going deep is the prized goal.

We tear apart and revel in the details rather than seeing the whole. My hunch is that we do this because the details are easier to deal with than the whole, since the whole often leaves us in the turmoil of our finiteness with too many tensions for our Greek-influenced minds.

This big fat Greek overemphasis on analysis has led us to create divisions that aren't in the Bible. Modern Christian literature is soaked in the use of "Evangelism and Discipleship," yet that division is a modern invention, not a first-century expression of Christianity. We find Jesus discipling people to conversion rather than evangelizing them. Our unexamined mind-set drives us to understand rather than obey and leads us to take apart things that Jesus never intended to be separated. A desire to know rather than obey sidetracks us into the development and distribution of materials that don't even fit into what Jesus has called us to.

We've spent countless dollars and hours training Christians to share their faith, equipping them to do mental battle with the nonbelieving world, all the while fostering the fallacy that if people understand, they will believe. That is so different from Jesus in Luke 10, sending His disciples out. They were instructed to simply engage the community, and where they found someone willing, to offer simple spiritual statements—"Peace to the house"—and to stay there. Certainly, conversation ensued about why they were there so that the subject of Jesus rolled into plain view. Remember from the passage that Jesus was about to go to these places. The disciples' job was to witness, not persuade.

That Greek mind-set may also contribute to the failure of Bible translators to accurately deliver the meaning of biblical words to modern culture. Take the words *faith* or *believe*. The Greek word *pistis* is used frequently in the second half of the Bible. One hundred years ago *faith* or *believe* may have indicated a high degree of action, but in the modern world the active nature of these words have been sucked dry. They have come to mean little other than a mental assent to a set of facts. The word *trust*, which is a legitimate translation of *pistis*, has the active meaning of living as if something is true. A simple replacement of *trust* with *faith* at every use of the word *pistis* in the Bible could shade the meaning for the modern world in a biblical direction.

The importance of words was brought home to me when a friend of mine complained about the translation of the word *observe* in the King James Bible rather than *obey*. To him, Americans observe holidays and speed limits (right?). To him, *observe* had little weight, or at least much less than *obey*. I mentioned this in passing while another friend, who was British, was in my presence. The Brit protested vehemently. In England, the word *observe* still has teeth. A Brit who is told to observe something pays close attention. The subtleties of words make such a big difference. If modern-day Christianity read *trust* instead of *believe* or *faith*, where would we be? I TRUST that we'd be further than we are in the endeavor to take the good news to the ends of the earth.

This translation issue affects even the way we share the good news. Most of our efforts are aimed at persuading people to believe rather than giving them opportunities to trust. Scot McKnight addresses this issue in *King Jesus Gospel*. He suggests that we've created a community of consumers who are brand loyal but who fail to understand the nature of allegiance when it comes to what Jesus asked us to do. Because our attempts at sharing the gospel hover around getting people to believe in Jesus' death on the cross, we fail to help people understand that this is not about adding another belief to your life—analysis. This is about exchanging the organizing principle you currently have for God who came in the flesh—synthesis. Jesus is the new King, and because of His life, death, and resurrection, you have the privilege of living in His kingdom under His kingship.

> **If modern-day Christianity read *trust* instead of *believe* or *faith*, where would we be?**

All is not lost in our world. Harbingers like Richard Foster and Dallas Willard have called us back to disciplines that engage not only the mind but also the body in our spiritual journeys. The rediscovery of disciplines such as fasting and silence bring the body back to the spiritual journey and reunite what God never intended to be separated. Yet we are unaware of the mechanism guiding our practices;

therefore, we fail to figure out how to make obedience to all the commands of Jesus the cornerstone in disciple-making.

The challenge is to expose our wetness, a painful and tedious process to see how we've allowed this Greek way of thinking to separate us from the truth. It starts by giving the thought a chance to live by asking ourselves, "Could this be true? Do I have a great big fat Greek way of thinking?" These questions coupled with perseverance will lead to a new way of seeing that, in turn, will take us to a new way of leading.

TEACHING BY ANALYSIS

This new way of leading is a discovery process that has disciple-making disciples being facilitators to help people find God and His will by reading the Bible. This broaches a very dangerous topic—one that threatens the essence of the identity of many Christian leaders and directly challenges the Greek mind-set where the accumulation and dissemination of knowledge is celebrated. In the discovery process, our facilitators refrain from answering questions about the Bible, and they use questions to drive people back to the text itself. There is little room for directive teaching in the discovery process. People are encouraged to hear from God by reading the Bible for themselves and obeying it.

This usually starts a fight. "What? No directive teaching? How will they learn then?" Just wait a minute. Let's take a deep breath and look at this concept of teaching. There is no doubt that modern Christianity relies on subject-matter experts. They can be seen in the bookstores and on the conference stages, read in the blogosphere, and heard on podcast. But even on a local level, Christian communities are organized around subject-matter experts whether they are called church planter, pastor, minister, missional community

People are encouraged to hear from God by reading the Bible for themselves and obeying it.

leader, house church leader, elder, deacon, Sunday school teacher, or something else.

In good Greek tradition, we've displayed our love of knowledge by arranging our organizations and ministry training to amass knowledge in people who are tasked with passing it on by lecturing to others. This exchange of knowledge is mistakenly called "discipleship." If signs of a reproductive faith were prevalent, I wouldn't have written this book. It is no secret that we haven't been able to crack the disciple-making disciple code.

Why? Among other things, it may be our misunderstanding of the word *teach*. I remember hearing Howard Hendricks say on more than one occasion, "The teacher hasn't taught until the learner has learned." Hendricks was the master of the quip, but what if this quip became the measuring stick of anyone one claiming to be a Christian teacher in any context? Remember, he didn't say they heard but specified that the learner has learned.

If teachers knew that success was counted by how many of those listening actually learned, it would radically alter the landscape of teaching. Yet it seems that we hold Christian teachers to far less stringent standards. We are willing to hold public school teachers to higher standards by requiring that their remuneration be tied to their students' performance on standardized tests. Yet people who handle eternal truth are held to a lesser standard. Instead, we celebrate those who merely hold our attention and are humorous, energetic, passionate, knowledgeable, and relevant.

Without revealing myself as a Greek and Hebrew nerd, let me assert that both the Hebrew and Greek words for *teaching* hold a causative meaning. That's the way we get the word *teach* from "cause to learning."[4] So when Isaiah asks, "Who has directed the Spirit of the Eternal One? Can anyone claim to be His advisor?" (40:13), he means who can cause Yahweh to learn. Of course, this is a rhetorical question because the Infinite cannot be taught!

Please understand, I am not arguing that every use of the word *teach* in the Bible means "cause to learn." But if teaching is simple lecturing, delivering content, the transfer of knowledge from one person to another, it doesn't qualify under the biblical standards for teaching. If teaching is training others to use the same labels for concepts, then we are defining *teaching* as facilitating memorization. Memorizing doesn't scratch deep enough to engage life change. You shouldn't take comfort as a teacher just because I accept your labels and regurgitate them back to you.

Transformation takes place deep inside a person where no teacher can manipulate. So, as a teacher, if I am going to participate with God the Spirit in the teaching learning process, I need to aim deep, much deeper than the memory, and clothe myself with a great humility because I am attempting to operate in an area where I am blind.

There is a transaction between God the Spirit, eternal truth, and the human soul that I am not privy to, nor do I necessarily under- stand it. So what is my role as a teacher? Am I a lamplighter bringing light? A gardener cultivating? Physical trainer strengthening? Potter shaping? Dietician feeding? Builder constructing?

Our role is determined not by our gifts, desires, and passions but by the nature of the transformation process. Jesus was clear that we are defiled not by what goes in but by what comes out (Matt. 15:11). The change in reality starts within. This can be compared to a color-blind person and a non-color-blind person looking at a stop sign. If asked, "What color do you see?" each person would have a different answer. Both answers are true from each person's perspective.

Or if I said, "My grandmother likes climbing vines." Do I have an athletic grandmother or one with a green thumb? Most grand- mothers don't climb vines, but to be certain you must search deeper.

Meaning starts deep within someone. Our personal experiences and reactions to them create catagories of understanding that are deeply personal. No one besides the person themselves can put this there with any certainty or effectiveness. If I assign meaning from somewhere inside me, we can't speak of objectivity, only objectivities. I have an objectivity, and you have an objectivity. Every person brings his or her objectivity to the table. If that is the reality of the teaching environment, monologues and lectures might be the least effective way to create life transformation, since it is one objectivity attempting to address multiple objectivities without any dialogue.

Teaching as a transfer of information is hardly what Paul had in mind when he challenged us to be renewed by the transforming of our minds (Rom. 12:2). But we are stuck in a paradigm. When we see the word *kyrusso*, the Greek word for *proclaim*, we almost always have a picture of someone delivering a monologue, persuading others to believe or obey. In that moment, we jump from the first-century meaning to modern-day forms and read the word as a lone person speaking to a group.

> **Teaching as a transfer of information is hardly what Paul had in mind when he challenged us.**

The word *proclaim* means, "to publicly announce religious truths and principles while urging acceptance and compliance."[5] Immediately we picture large groups of people sitting in rows. But is that really in this word? The word does not define group size; it is simply "public." To urge compliance doesn't imply a lone speaker bringing a crowd to a point of conviction with emotion. There are multiple ways to urge compliance.

Adults have a high degree of commitment to their own conclusions and a low degree of commitment to conclusions given to them by others. This is not new information. Unfortunately, most attempts at education and spiritual transformation in the church, as well as those attempting to reach people far from God, start with a set of conclusions. We attempt to transfer those conclusions to others through persuasion, in monologues, most of them delivered in passionate sincerity.

This process is exacerbated by cultural dynamics in the West. We live in a world of persuasion. At every turn there is a flat surface with a persuading message, attempting to get us to sign up, subscribe, purchase, or pay attention to stuff. Persuasion abounds, from the time of *Mad Men*, AMC's drama that looks inside advertising in the 1960s, to what Google has done to advertising in the digital age. It is no wonder that we resist being sold because it feels as if everyone is out to sell us something most of our waking hours. This affects those of us attempting to woo a world that doesn't even know it lacks a vital relationship with a heavenly Father. Couching the good news in selling methods starts us down an unproductive path in the West.

We know that the more students participate the more they learn. The tragedy is that we are caught in a system that worships form rather than function! There is little room to do things differently than we've done them before. In fact, it may not be an exaggeration to suggest there is fear of losing control if we change.

The hardcore truth is that teaching through lectures is an inadequate weapon for spiritual warfare. I must aim inside people for transformation to take place.

TEACHING BY SYNTHESIS

So I like a new definition of *teaching*: helping people make meaning. This moves me from a lecturer to a learning-environment designer.

When I begin to think about catalyzing spiritual transformations, I have God, the Spirit, the eternal truth, and the perceptions of those I am working with. Failing to see the perceptions of others as a dynamic variable in the teaching/learning equation will relegate me to nothing more than a talking head who loves the sound of his own voice.

If I engage the learners' reality in partnership with a Triune God and eternal truth, they might never be the same. But I have to aim deeper than just their ears. I need to design experiences in which they can make meaning of God's eternal truth.

A monologue disseminates information, and information is needed, but this is only the beginning of the transformational process. It is a travesty that for most followers of Christ this is also the only step in their discipling process. Sit, listen, eat, go home. Breaking that pattern will take work.

Humans, and especially adults, place a high degree of value on equilibrium. It goes by different monikers like peace, comfort, balance, or stability. This state is achieved by developing patterns of thinking that help us explain the reality around us. We develop affection for these patterns and hold on to them because they serve us well most of the time.

To see people change, grow, and rethink life, we need to disturb that equilibrium. But that doesn't give me carte blanche on the human level to violate human sensibilities. There is a delicate balance between maintaining trust in a relationship and bringing opportunities for growth that disturb the status quo. It is helpful in the spiritual journey that God the Spirit is active in someone genuinely interested in connecting with him.

In the spiritual realm we have a divine partner. God the Spirit is in the middle of all of our activities. We aren't the only ones engaged in promoting the good news. Jesus promised in the Great Commission that He is with us.

Once disturbed, people will find their way to balance. It is uncanny how much energy humans will expend to find their way back to equilibrium. Only this time as they seek peace, the discomfort in their lives has affected their patterns of thinking such that they have created a new level of stability. It is called growth, and every living thing experiences it.

The educational process looks much like the process of physical growth. There is equilibrium, then something disturbs the peace and creates chaos. The chaos brings the old order into question. The old categories aren't necessarily working. The chaos creates new pieces of data to process, and a new order begins to develop. As a result, the organism reorganizes at a higher level—more fit, stronger, and ready to do it again.

This process describes how exercise benefits health. It is the stuff of great athletic training in every sport. It describes how we gain emotional health, learn new skills, extinguish old habits, and encourage our bodies to change for the better. And it is the process of teaching by synthesis.

My wife, Candy, and I met Bob and Jennifer on the city park tennis courts. She was in her late twenties and Bob was in his early fifties. Candy and Jennifer hit it off right away and began to spend time together. Jennifer had a spiritual thirst but Bob was not interested. As far as he was concerned, he had his spiritual life together and didn't need anyone telling him how to live his life.

Bob had been divorced twice and Jennifer had never been married. He provided a stable, seasoned influence that she loved, so maintaining a romantic relationship and living together worked well for them. They didn't feel the need to rush into anything "official."

In another phase in our lives, Candy and I would have addressed the living situation right up front or maybe even kept our distance because of it, but that was no longer the case. So we had dinner, played tennis, and pursued the spiritual journey with Jennifer. It wasn't long before Candy and Jennifer began to read the Bible together. Jennifer's thirst for God was apparent, but the more she grew in her faith the more uncomfortable Bob became. We didn't spend a lot of time with them, but when we did it was apparent that

Jennifer was devouring the Bible even on her own. One day, much to Bob's dismay, she came to us and said, "I think that Bob and I need to stop having sex." She was a rather blunt person.

As we inquired about how she came to that decision, she blamed God. From reading the Bible she came to the conclusion that sex was a joy reserved for marriage and she and Bob were not married, nor did they ever intend to get married. They were pursuing a lifetime together as very close friends with benefits.

"What are you going to do?" Candy asked.

She thought for a moment and said, "There's not a chance that we could live in the same house and not have sex, so I guess I need to move out."

"That's a pretty aggressive move on your part. Are you sure you want to do that?" I asked.

I'll never forget Jennifer's response, "If you were the one telling me I needed to move out, that would be one thing, but when God tells me something, I know I'd better do it."

Jennifer and Bob separated. It not only broke Bob's heart more than any of us realized it would but also softened his heart, allowing him to begin a spiritual pursuit. He, too, began to read the Bible and dismantle the self-shaped religion that he used to keep spiritual people away. It was not clear at first if this new found interest in spiritual things was aimed at getting himself back into Jennifer's life or not. But as time went on and their relationship didn't heal, Bob still showed genuine spiritual and personal growth.

Both Bob and Jennifer continued their spiritual journeys. Since the relationship Candy and I had with them was casual, neither developed a dependency on us in their early spiritual journey. We didn't spend hours sharing our wisdom or answering questions. We always pointed them back to the Bible and God as their primary source for growth. Their early spiritual experiences gave them the confidence in hearing from God.

As Christians, we know a lot about the Bible and can share wisdom and insight into the spiritual journey, but we often ignore the fact that this sharing can develop a dependency that is crippling to the replication process. It might take years for some people to gain the Bible knowledge and experience you have. But is gaining knowledge the goal? If that is what is needed before disciples can make disciples, no wonder we have more hell-bound people today than ever in the history of humankind.

An illusion of control exists among Christians. Common Christian wisdom assumes that we need a trained subject-matter expert to disciple so as to avoid certain negative experiences, namely heresy. The humor in this is that we've had trained subject-matter experts all throughout history and we haven't avoided heresy. In fact, a cursory survey of church history reveals that most major heresies in the past two thousand years find their source in trained clergy and not the untrained.

Too often this assertion of heresy is brought by those who either ignore or are uninformed about the history of the good news. Christianity's aberrations find their origins in the academics where that great big fat Greek way of thinking rules. When you refuse to accept the revealed tensions of the Bible, it leads to dissection of the infinite using finite logic and gives birth to heresy. Some things are not possible to explain (Deut. 29:29).

FROM TEACHERS TO LEARNING DESIGNERS

Teaching needs to take on a new dynamic. We need to move from trafficking in information transfer and instead become learning designers. If people won't act on our conclusions, we need to stop telling them what to think. Better yet, if we want to influence others with the truth then why not begin suggesting what they ought to be thinking about? Here again is a new definition of *teaching*: helping people make meaning.

Instead of using deductive strategies that state our conclusion, then spending time defending, why not bring people into close quarters with a revelation that creates discomfort in their paradigms? I've spent hours defending the exclusivity of Christianity. Nothing I've done compares to the moments I've taken people to John 14:6 and we've read it together. Jesus says, "I am the path, the truth, and the energy of life. No one comes to the Father except through Me." I am always amazed at the response I get. They will take it from Jesus but argue with me. Maybe that is why Jesus said, "My sheep respond as they hear My voice" (John 10:27).

I have a lot of confidence in my grasp of the facts, culture, history, and theology contained in the Bible. I paid a lot of money for my education, so it shouldn't come as a surprise that I like to display that knowledge and regale people with my grasp of biblical minutiae. The truth is, sharing knowledge just isn't that effective in catalyzing change in people's lives.

However, when I give up my front row seat and let them sit there so they can get face-to-face with God, something amazing happens. They don't depend on me for answers to their questions. They get firsthand knowledge of God. The empowerment factor is stunning when you let people know that they can have a face-to-face connection with God without having all that "secret" knowledge about the Bible. Sometimes it feels as if we've created a new Gnosticism just to keep people in their places. We overturned that heresy thousands of years ago!

There is freedom and power when I remove myself from a pre-Reformational ministry mind-set and refuse to create dependencies on individuals or institutions. Teaching people to relate to and depend on God is difficult without creating earthly dependencies, but it is possible.

Even Socrates, the great Greek philosopher, said, "I cannot teach anybody anything, I can only make them think." He understood what many of us don't. Answering questions doesn't transform. It might transfer information, but it doesn't make fundamental shifts inside a person.

The great teachers of the world knew the power of questions. They knew that if the teacher is doing all the work, very little life change is happening. But when the student is doing most of the work, something significant is in process.

Most of us subject-matter experts are afflicted with the curse of knowledge. We are overly certain and mistakenly assume that others will come to certainty through our actions. Or at least we assume they have the conceptual patterns, vocabulary, and world-view that will allow them to understand. But often, the listener doesn't draw the same conclusions that we do because this person doesn't have the same genetics, upbringing, personality, patterns of relating, or information as we do.

If we are going to regain momentum toward the Great Com-mission, we are in desperate need of repentance from the overcon-fidence we have in ourselves as teachers. We are a small and infinite part of a grand divine scheme. We should do our part but not presume that we are more powerful than we are.

When my children were little we bought them walkie-talkies. I have four children, so over the years we bought several sets. One rainy day when they were in late grade-school days, out of bore-dom, they found several pieces of the sets from yesteryear. After scavenging batteries from the TV remotes they set about to play. The only problem was that they had one each of two different types of walkie-talkie.

Listening to them sit in their bedrooms to test them out became quite comical.

"Can you hear me?"

"Not through the walkie-talkie."

Now louder, "Can you hear me now?"

And so it went until the max vocal volume had been reached. They had a problem and maybe you've already guessed what it was. The walkie-talkies were on different frequencies. It didn't matter if the volume knobs on the walkie-talkies went to eleven because being on different frequencies meant they were not going to connect. No amount of power would make a difference.

Is it delusions of grandeur or innocent passion that causes us to presume more power than we really possess? Our heroes are passionate, theologically astute, and media savvy. They are amazing communicators. To be like them is the secret hope of every theologue in training. I know because I was one. But Jesus didn't call us to be communicators, He called us to be disciple-makers. Oh for the day that our heroes are those who are catalyzing self-replicating generations of disciple-making disciples and not just highly gifted people who can hold our attention for an hour.

What does it mean to move from an information transfer to a learning design model? There are several initial presumptions. First, start where the learner is, not where you are; second, let them drive the agenda; and third, allow them to be the author, not you.

START WHERE THE LEARNER IS

Where else would you start if not where the learner is? Such a simple presumption, yet when we evangelize, we often fail to ascertain someone's worldview, concepts of authority, and previous religious history. We want to know what they think about Jesus. It's great if exploring their history is a good jumping off point, but usually it is not. Our interest usually focuses on finding an opening to explain the facts of the cross.

Starting where the learners are means using language that they can understand. Christians need to talk about their spiritual journeys in language that the average non-churchgoer can understand. Our use of "insider" language communicates a cultural imperialism. It is no wonder that the pre-Christian crowd is allergic to us. Have you tried to audit your vocabulary to see what biblical allusions you use that are not in common use? The blood of Jesus is dear to us because it represents the ultimate sacrifice for the unworthy. But the phrase itself sounds gross to those outside our culture. Take something as simple as Old Testament and New Testament. The average biblically-illiterate person has no idea what the Old Testament is. The litmus test should be whether you can explain what God is up to in this world using language understood by people far from God.

LET THE LEARNER DRIVE THE AGENDA

The only one who comes to a learning situation with a need is the learner. God doesn't have a need to be related to, the truth doesn't have a need to be trusted, and a teacher doesn't have a need to teach. Since the learner brings the need, the environment should be designed to allow them to drive the agenda.

The environment needs to be structured in such a way that, not only is the learner driving the agenda, he or she is the one doing most of the work. Force-feeding using a subject matter expert allows for a great deal of passivity on the part of the learner. The typical information delivery mode never determines the quality of the soil in which the seed is planted. Giving the learner the opportunity to drive the agenda exposes the quality of spiritual interest. It is his or her questions that need to be answered. If there are no questions, then we might be working with the wrong person.

ALLOW THE LEARNER TO BE THE AUTHOR

In a learning environment the energy of the learner is a good litmus test as to whether the subject matter and the need of the learner are in sync. Questions, the learner's questions, are a good gauge of that energy. The discovery process is designed to allow the learner to put his eyes on the Bible and come to conclusions he is willing to act on.

Because the average person accepts his own conclusions much more readily and deeper than conclusions given to him, efficiency in the learning process demands we create situations where he comes to his own conclusions. I am always humbled by those being discipled into the family of God—those who, when confronted by the truth, aren't bashful about coming to obedient statements that would challenge even most followers of Christ.

CONCLUSION

We need to listen to Jesus. Jesus said, "Teach to obey!" Our disciple-making efforts should aim at obedience, not knowledge. We don't need more teachers; we need more learning designers to build obedience-focused, accountable disciple-making experiences.

If we are going to invite people to the table to read the Bible and discover what God has to say about life, we need to provide the starting points in the Bible. We need to know the main obstacles that exist between the audience we are attempting to connect with and the Creator God.

Obedience-focused, discovery-based, multiplicative disciple-making has moved Shoal Creek in that direction. No subject-matter experts exist there to answer everyone's questions. We have a simple, repeatable process in place that gives all participants the opportunity to learn, repeat, and replicate their lives in others.

Shoal Creek has identified eight questions that need to be addressed when choosing portions of the Bible for someone to read and hear from God:

1. Where did everything come from?

2. Is there any meaning to this life?

3. Who do I listen to for authoritative advice on life?

4. Does human history lead anywhere, or is it all in vain since death is merely the end?

5. Where do we look to determine what is good or bad, right or wrong?

6. Why don't I ever feel good enough?

7. Who is Jesus and how should I understand Him in relationship to God?

8. What is my place in what God is up to in this world?

From these we've devised a route through the Bible that starts with answering these questions. By asking people to come and read the Bible and find out what God has to say about life, we see them begin to relate to God as a son or daughter would relate to a father and continue on the lifelong journey of being a disciple-making disciple. In fact, we accompany people on *seven* journeys. In part 2 of this book, chapters 5–8 tell the story of the Shoal Creek plan, how it developed (chap. 5), how it works (chap. 6), the seven journeys toward being a disciple-making disciple (chap. 7), and lessons for leaders (chap. 8).

PART TWO

THE SOLUTION

HYBRID CHURCH

It all started with a dream. Though I am a graduate of Dallas Theological Seminary, a school in which most graduates are theologically opposed to dreaming when it relates to God, I had a dream in which God was very active.

Since the beginning of Shoal Creek Community Church, I prayed regularly for the 300 thousand people within a thirty-minute drive from our meeting space. (We've since changed our location, and now we pray for the 2.3 million people in the Kansas City metro area.) I would read 1 Timothy 2 and plead with God, "Your heart is to see them come to you. How do I get their attention? How can I convince them that this is a safe place to explore a very dangerous message?"

We had recently acquired what I felt could be a catalyst for the sudden surge in growth I had been praying for. After our four-year pursuit, God had finally made available for us an old church building that sat less than a mile from the intersection of I-35 and I-435 in the northern suburbs of Kansas City, providing all three of the key ingredients in an excellent church campus—location, location, location.

During this process I had been reading Roland Allen's *The Spontaneous Expansion of the Church and the Causes which Hinder It.* Allen suggested that if our strategy can't attain what Jesus commanded us to do then we ought to change our strategy. This might have been the blasting cap for the situation I was about to experience. This thought was rolling around in my head and pounding in my heart as the dream started.

In the dream, God answered my prayer. Three hundred thousand descended on Shoal Creek's campus on Sunday morning. At first it was glorious—families getting in cars, single moms packing up kids, people rolling out of bars, exotic dancers just getting off their shifts, assembly workers coming to a church meeting rather than heading to breakfast, a beautiful scene of humanity in search of God.

But then the dream turned to a nightmare. Kansas City, like any other city, doesn't have the infrastructure to accommodate 300 thousand people in one place. So more quickly than I appreciated, traffic congestion appeared. Ribbons of concrete became a twisted mess, a sea of automobiles moved at less than a snail's pace because the highway system wouldn't facilitate them all getting to this small place. Realistically, we can accommodate only 450 cars and 1,200 people at a time!

The traffic jams were so exasperating that instead of persevering, people turned around and went home. The fire of spiritual intrigue was doused by inadequate infrastructure. A mass of humanity was prevented from connecting with a place that would nurture their spiritual interest.

This dream-turned-nightmare revealed that my strategy and my prayers were mismatched. In 1995, a small group people who would later become Shoal Creek went to a conference in South Barrington, Illinois, to learn about building a church for those far from God. We got excited because all of us cut our teeth in college on highly evangelistic ministries. Our hope was to recover that spiritual passion for reaching and discipling people who had yet to connect with God.

Hearing Bill Hybels's impassioned plea for building a church for the unchurched lit a fire that still burns today. The group has grown, mainly through conversion growth. We don't attract many Christians because we don't do musical worship on Sunday. For eight years we faithfully pursued that strategy, inviting our friends, neighbors, and workmates to join us in pursuing a spiritual journey.

As I mentioned at the beginning of the book, this is more of a journal than a manual. I don't intend to convince you to become like us in the *what* and *how*. Our tactical decisions are driven by some very clear strategic conclusions. They are the *whys* of who we are, who our audience is and what we do.

The energy you might feel to persuade is not to do things like we do, but to consider thinking differently. Besides, we are not on the list of the fastest-growing churches in America, far from it! We don't have the numbers that would impress anyone. Although we've wanted to be on the "Success Train" of American church planting, God has blessed us with small steady growth.

My hope is to help you understand how we have taken the Great Commission and applied it to cultural environment. It is *why* we do what we do that is important not the techniques or strategies that we use to carry it out. Friedrich Nietzsche said, "He who has a why to live for can bear almost any how." That is my agenda, to get you to *why*.

From day one we were very clear: we don't feed people; we teach them to feed themselves. When I think of my teenagers standing in the kitchen asking to be fed, I can't help but feel that only the worst parent would feed them. Teens are old enough to feed themselves; if they don't possess that skill then it is time to teach them.

I know you are going to throw Bible verses at me that talk about feeding His sheep, or as *The Voice* translates the verses, "Take care of my lambs," "shepherd my sheep," and "look after my sheep" (John

21:15–17). But could I just get you to think with me for a moment about what that means?

What we practice in our churches is handing out regurgitated truth every Sunday under the guise of teaching. It is as if someone chews the food for us to make it more easily digestible and then ladles it out so we can slurp it down.

Is that what Jesus had in mind when He spoke to Peter? Did the shepherd take the sheep to the field, pull the grass with his hands, and chew it up into a gooey green slime? Would he drool that green slimy mixture into a bottle or small bowl then open the sheep's mouth and pour it in? Of course not!

What Jesus said to Peter in John 21 doesn't support that imagery at all. The shepherd takes the sheep to where the food is, and the sheep eat on their own. "Feed my sheep" (KJV) is more akin to "show them," "help them discover how," or "teach them to feed themselves" than it is to the picture we have today.

We create enormous dependencies when we imply that we will feed people. The church world rocked the day Bill Hybels said, "We made a mistake."[1] It wasn't a repudiation of the Seeker Movement, but it was an admission that every church should have had the guts to make. Willow Creek taught people to depend on the church for their primary spiritual growth and wasn't able to deliver on that promise. No church is.

When you create dependencies on people or institutions for spiritual growth, you make the gospel heavy and unable to move swiftly. It is an injustice to the Great Commission to load Jesus' strategy with manmade burdens. As Jesus taught in Matthew 23, our dependency is not on rabbis, fathers, or teachers, but on God Himself.

We had a classic attractional church that found a way to attract the nonbelieving world and keep Christians from filling up the chairs. Unfortunately, our strategy could only accommodate six to ten thousand people on our campus, if we got really creative. We'd have been excited about those numbers had I not convinced people to pray for 300 thousand.

We've always been able to think beyond our current strategies because our core function, make disciple-making disciples, has always driven our strategies. We regularly asked what needed to be done, not just what we could do. How could we reach the 300 thousand we were praying for? After reading all the current books on church strategy, endlessly searching the internet, and making countless phone calls, we went on a road trip to figure out who could lead us to the promised land.

As we started on a search for a scalable model for making disciples—a strategy that would allow us to grow without being restricted by facilities or economics—we went through all of the typical strategies in vogue. Our search became really frustrating because at every stop we hit a wall. Was what we did on Sundays not easily replicable? Multi-site, Rapid Church Multiplication, traditional church planting, video venues, house church networks—all of them required changing what was already moderately successful and didn't promise the same success.

> Our core function, make disciple-making disciples, has always driven our strategies.

I remember asking the Leadership Network folks if they could point us toward a church like ours doing multi-site. They couldn't. That might be different today, but we seldom find churches like Shoal Creek. In fact, the response I usually get when I say, "We don't do musical worship on Sunday" is, "What do you do?"

Instead of musical worship songs on Sunday morning, we sing current songs by U2, Coldplay, Black Eyed Peas, Lorde, Simple Plan, Mumford and Sons, and just about anyone else you could mention. We struggle to keep our music team stocked with the talented volunteer musicians and vocalists we need. Plopping down three multi-sites just wasn't an option. We couldn't find the talent to do live music at these venues. Piping it over the internet or putting it on DVD on a one-week delay just didn't get the same texture and feel in a room.

Since our thinking causes us to start where those who don't have a family relationship with God are, we use their music and their life issues as a starting point. We navigate back to the biblical truth from there. It is our hope that Sundays will start a discussion, not deliver a conclusion.

BHOJPURI

While pursuing this path, I kept notes that I didn't want to leave my visual reach on a whiteboard. Up in the corner, I wrote "Bhojpuri." It was a reminder that someday I needed to explore this story from northern India that sounded as if it had some evangelistic inflation to the numbers used in the story. Frustration at every turn made that little word stand out even more. Thoughts like, *that's India* or *that can happen there, but not here* swirled through my brain. But desperation is an amazing motivator, so I jumped into the story to see if I could expose the exaggeration and erase this word from my whiteboard.

The report I read looked as if it came from credible people. It had been compiled by six different organizations that didn't have a vested interest in providing exaggerated stories to the church. The numbers are insignificant in some ways but absolutely astounding: 100 thousand people baptized in 2007 alone. A minimum of forty thousand churches representing at a minimum 1.5 million people in fourteen years! These are numbers that would make even the most skeptical person take a second look, if only to disprove them.

Right away we discovered several key values that we held in common with what was happening in Bhojpuri. We:

- ✿ work with people who are not in a family relationship with God,

- disciple people to conversion by getting them reading the Bible rather than trying to evangelize them,

- focus on obedience with accountable structure rather than knowledge, and

- trust everyone to be a disciple-maker.

But this was not an attracting style, so we wondered whether it would fit with our model. Did we need to stop what we were doing and change directions? A period of creative confusion set in and formed the primordial soup from which we would hear another word from God.

TEST DRIVE

A simple test drive became a spiritual muse in the process. My octogenarian in-laws wanted a new car, even though neither of them could drive at the time! You just don't argue with eighty-plus-year-old people. A friend owned a car they were looking at, so we borrowed it for a test drive. Until that day, I had never driven a hybrid car.

Being ever practical, my mother-in-law wanted to stop by the grocery store to pick up a few things during the test drive, so I parked just outside the door of her favorite market and waited while she ran in. Thirty minutes later she emerged with two bags of groceries and climbed back into the passenger seat of the hybrid.

It was then the drama began. I hadn't turned the car off because the hybrid engine didn't seem to be running, so when my mother-in-law returned to the car I didn't have to turn it back on. When the car started to move forward, it was a strange sensation to experience movement without hearing an engine revving. It must have been equally as strange for the lady who walked right in front of the moving car. Fortunately, the brakes are conventional. They worked exceptionally well and sprang into action, creating a threatening screech as soon as I slammed my foot onto the pedal.

I'm sure that it never occurred to the lady coming out of the store that a car not making a sound could be a threat to her life. She grew up in a world where cars made sounds; engines revved when they moved, and especially when they moved from a stand-still.

Her world had now changed! Her old paradigm had brought her into harm's way, and her survival depended on changing her thinking and behavior. Hybrid cars that possess both gas engines that rev and electric engines that don't had entered her world. No longer could she count on hearing a car coming at her. She must now understand that cars may move silently, propelled by an electric engine.

This moment gave birth to a new way of thinking about how I did church.

This moment gave birth to a new way of thinking about how I did church. As I have described, in 1994, I began a journey to establish a Willow-Creek model church. After eleven years, Shoal Creek was approaching eight hundred people and growing. It didn't take an Einsteinian mathematician to figure out that our current facility had an expiration date that was swiftly approaching.

Having planted the church from six people in my living room, I was sure that I only had one church plant in me. The clawing for viability while raising a family left trace elements of stress, fatigue, and aging. It was as if I had been trying to light a fire under the church and subsequently discovered that all of my matches were spent. This frustration catalyzed a journey to find a scalable strategy that would reduce the dependence on facilities and allow us to continue to aggressively participate in seeing the lost found.

My experience with the hybrid car and the principles applied to it drove me back to the Bible. This was a reread for me, which made it deceptively difficult. Never was I more aware of the cultural bias that I brought to the Bible. The forms that have developed over centuries had to be submitted to the functions that the Bible laid out. The practices with which Jesus launched the first Disciple-Making Movement had to erase my paradigms of tradition.

Now a holy collision was set up: a viable biblical strategy to make disciples who would multiply at viral rates, irrespective of traditionally trained leaders and adequate facilities, and a church with an aggressive heart to reach those not yet vitally connected with their heavenly Father through His Son.

A HYBRID DISCIPLE-MAKING STRATEGY

My engagement in the Bhojpuri story caused me to ask some hard questions and reread some familiar passages in the Bible, such as Matthew 28. A fresh reading created new insight. Not only was I responsible for making disciples, but my disciples were responsible for making disciples as well. A subtly profound conclusion! So in effect, the Great Commission requires me to make disciple-making disciples.

The sobering reality set in on me: methods are important. In the discipling process, if I were going to make disciple-making disciples, that is, obey the Great Commission, I needed to choose methods that were simple and repeatable by people with different personalities and types of giftedness. I was responsible for baptizing disciples and teaching them to obey with methods that they could use to continue making disciple-making disciples.

So at Shoal Creek we changed our measure of success. No longer would we be satisfied with simply making disciples. All of our activities and energy would now be measured against a new understanding of the Great Commission. Only when our disciples were making disciples could we say that we had reached the finish line!

This realization along with the Bhojpuri story created a collision of epic proportion. How would a church based on attracting people and designed to meet the strongest felt need fit together with a viral disciple-making strategy? Two unique and somewhat competing strategies existing alongside one another, a HYBRID!

Yes, the car I was driving that almost flattened an innocent grocery-shopper gave me the inspiration to put these two strategies together. The car had two unique power sources in it, gas and electric. The gas engine is old technology that is well understood and commonly used. The electric engine, although not new, is a recent application to the automobile and particularly the presence of both gas and electric alongside each other in the same automobile.

We trust the gas engine because we know it, yet of late we are more aware than ever of the dangers it poses to our world. So the electric technology has been put alongside it to create better efficiencies. The two technologies are distinct in every way—the principles on which they are built, the dynamics of producing power, the parts and principles of maintenance. Yet they cooperate with one another when they serve a common mission, to propel the car.

The hybrid car became a metaphor for Shoal Creek. On one side is the old attractional model—gas engine—inviting people each week to come discover a life that they've always wanted. On the other side a gospel planting model—electric engine—that equips people to move into their neighborhoods, workplaces, and relational networks with the life-changing truth of Jesus.

On one side, we ask people to invite their friends aggressively; on the other, we train people not to mention Shoal Creek unless asked. On one side, we have a group structure that organizes virtual strangers into small, biblically functioning communities. On the other, we exploit natural, relational connections to plant the gospel in obedience-focused groups.

Why do we do this? We've prayed for years that God would allow us to see our 300 thousand neighbors come to follow Jesus. I was allowed the privilege of experiencing what it would look like to have that prayer answered in a dream that quickly became a nightmare! We couldn't handle the answers to our prayers. So we allowed a holy collision to take place and entered a hybrid world. How did we do it? Awkwardly at first. The Western mind does not hold things in tension well, yet our world is held together at the atomic level by just such tension. So our hope was to tell a story long enough for people to begin to get it.

THE *S* CURVE

We decided not to roll this out like we would other new ideas. The counterintuitive nature of Disciple-Making Movements was something that couldn't be marketed; it had to be caught, not taught. So we took on the role of a revolutionary, and decided to think about how terrorist groups recruit and market themselves.

No doubt the word "terrorist" is a politically-charged word, and horrible acts of violence are committed by people with this label almost daily. Despite the horror terrorists perpetrate in our world, they are effective at moving people from disenfranchised to active participants, from a high dissatisfaction to disciples who are willing to strap bombs to themselves.

They look around the edges for people who are dissatisfied and vulnerable to a new and different way of reaching out. In small and achievable steps they make disciples of their hideous ideologies. Each step of the way people have actionable steps so that they literally "obey" their way into thinking as the organization they are being recruited to. But Jesus told us to be as wise as serpents and harmless as doves, and we would do well to pay attention to their recruiting strategies and not their tactics.

Academics have long understood this approach. Frank Hairgrove, in his 2011 PhD dissertation at the University of Wisconsin "Media Use in Conversion into Islamic Radicalism: Why This Person and Not That Person, Why Here, Why Now?" describes this incremental

Jesus told us to be as wise as serpents and harmless as doves.

process with the eye of a scientist. It is observable and measurable, therefore repeatable. It became a model for us.

In an attempt to find people ready to obey the Great Commission we discovered people who had a holy dissatisfaction. They knew the "church" could do and be more but were frustrated with lack or creativity and risk that seemed to be holding it back. As good "Christians" they sat passively waiting for "the church" to do something.

In an attempt to find people ready to obey the Great Commission we discovered people who had a holy dissatisfaction.

We focused on high-value targets: men and women who already had a demonstrated love and concern for their lost friends and relatives. These people had already exhausted conventional strategies by repeatedly extending invitations to their relational network. The repeated nature of these invitations over time was bordering on irritating, so they were ripe for a new and different way of reaching out. In fact, we discovered there was an approximate seven year "S curve" they all had in common.

The S curve describes most growth, organic and organizational. At the bottom is a distinct turn from downward to upward, signifying new life and steep growth. That growth continues for a period of time until there is a slowing at the peak. If something doesn't take place, the peak will evolve into another downturn. To avoid the downturn at the top, something needs to engage the descent to create another ascent.

I saw this firsthand when I took a ride in a hot air balloon. The gas burn created lift in the balloon as it rose swiftly, but the air cooled quickly. Just before the balloon lost momentum and began to drop, the pilot burned off more gas, providing heat and lift. If you drew the flight of a hot air balloon you would see that it is a series of "S's" as it gains altitude. Energy applied at the right time keeps the balloon ascending upward.

This pattern is somewhat like the evaluation given by Jesus to the church in Philadelphia when they obeyed God's direction but ran out of strength, "I know your deeds. See, I have placed before you an open door, which no one can shut. *I have done this* because you have limited strength, yet you have obeyed My word and have not denied My name" (Rev. 3:8).

That process was identified in numerous people, and they all had an approximate seven-year growth spurt in common. If we caught them at the right time, they were ready for something different because their relational networks were not expanding as fast as their ability to invite was.

DISCIPLE-MAKING MOVEMENTS

Enter a strategy learned from David Watson. David Watson along with Victor John was used by God to catalyze a movement among the Bhojpuri in India that is still going strong. One of Watson's disciples, David Broodryk who leads the TAN (Transform a Nation) Foundation and Accelerate Teams[2] provided the very first live training I attended.

Disciple-Making Movements (DMM) is a strategy that has six key characteristics:

1. God ordained,

2. Spirit dependent,

3. Bible centered,

4. obedience focused,

5. discovery based, and

6. disciple driven.

In brief, DMM turns average followers of Christ into event planners, rather than salesmen for Jesus, so that they can invite their friends, neighbors, and workmates into small groups designed to hear from God through reading the Bible, obeying what He says, and sharing it with their social networks.

CREATING THE HYBRID: COME *AND* GO

Our attractional Come strategy—our gasoline engine—was running well at Shoal Creek, but we understood that it didn't have the scalability to reach the more than 300 thousand in our area with the gospel. The new DMM/Go strategy—our electricity—did offer the possibility of reaching those 300 thousand and beyond. Putting the two together was no easy task. At times, they are seemingly opposite or even contradictory in nature. That is where the hybrid metaphor helps us communicate our vision. Like the hybrid auto, Shoal Creek has a mission. The car's mission is transportation, so the two different power sources serve that mission. The design allows each power source to work when it is most effective, cooperating despite their disparate technologies. Shoal Creek's mission is to turn spiritual seekers into a community of fully devoted followers of Christ. The two sides, Come/Go, serve to support that mission when each is most effective.

THE FIRST VALUE: LOVE PEOPLE WHO ARE FAR FROM GOD

From our anecdotal research, we have discovered that about 50 percent of our target audience will look for a spiritual beginning in an existing community of faith. There is something inside them that attaches safety and security to an established church, even if they have a negative attitude toward church people. So they are susceptible to a large meeting outreach that provides a safe place to be exposed to spiritual ideas.

The other 50 percent wouldn't come to a church service if their life depended on it. They have either had bad experiences with church, or they don't even have a category in their thinking for church. That is, when they think about spirituality, church is not one of the options that appears on their radar screen to deal with spiritual issues.

So the church's strategy would depend on its target. This is important to keep in mind. At the forefront of this metamorphosis is *a love for people who are far from God*. That passion drove us to the hybrid model and is the driving principle and first value behind this thinking. A passion for the lost then formed in us a desire to grow a church that focuses on people far from God, to bring Jesus' kingdom from heaven to earth.

THE SECOND VALUE: BUILD JESUS' KINGDOM ON EARTH

Although it sounds deliciously simple, there is a second fundamental decision we had to make regarding our Come/Go strategy. Growing an existing church and expanding Jesus' kingdom on this earth are not always good bedfellows. Once we adopted Disciple-Making Movements thinking, we had a second and very important value to live out. *We had to be willing to build Jesus' kingdom on earth even if it meant not growing our church's Sunday attendance.*

If you a leader of an existing church or church planter, please don't move through this idea too quickly. We are not paid as church leaders to lead people away from us or our church meetings. In fact we are measured by the number of people we attract. Recognizing and acting on the thought that building the Kingdom of Jesus and growing the church that we serve may be competing forces and they can cause potentially serious job-ending discussions.

It would have been easy to allow each side of the strategy to bleed into the other and use our in-home small groups as a way to grow attendance at Shoal Creek. But if our assumptions were right, an invitation to Shoal Creek on the Go side would be counterproductive. It would not help the 50 percent we prayed for to connect with God.

One day, I was sitting on my deck with a group of pastors discussing this issue. One of them looked at me and said, "If you aren't careful, you are going to work yourself out of a job." He saw the implication clearly: if the gospel moves away from individual churches such as Shoal Creek, it might threaten the viability of what we have traditionally called church.

I mentioned that I had a bucket list item—to work at Starbucks—that I would probably never get to. The implications he was drawing might make that possible, although I don't believe it will. But I am more than willing to see this happen if it means progress toward the fulfillment of the Great Commission in my lifetime.

It is no easy task to move the hybrid model from theory to practice.

It is no easy task to move the hybrid model from theory to practice. It requires "bimodal" thinking skills. Bimodal thinking consists of holding competing ideas in tension without jettisoning either.

To be a bimodal thinker is to be both logical and intuitive, big picture and detail oriented, near and far looking. Holding these competing outlooks in tension becomes a valuable asset. Although there is an objective picture of the hybrid strategy that appears clean and clear-cut, the practice is not always so.

The cultural landscape of the West is a "churched" culture. Despite all those sounding the alarms of post modernism, millennial evacuation and the rise of the "nones," something exists in the psyche of those, at least in the United States, that will always make the big box on the corner a viable place to pursue God. The vitality of that viability will be determined by those in the big box's ability to provide safe connections for a very dangerous message.

Typical communication and marketing channels might be the best source through which to launch the Come strategy. But the Go strategy is so counterintuitive, especially to people who have "churched genes," that pushing it through a loudspeaker produces disappointing results.

When the phrase "churched genes" is used, it doesn't necessarily refer to people who grew up in church. Shoal Creek began with the typical "church for the unchurched" mantra. It didn't take long to discover there are very few truly unchurched people in the United States. Certainly that number is growing, but our culture has a "churched" quality to it. Getting people to believe that legitimate spiritual communities can exist apart from buildings and budgets is not as easy as one might think, even when reaching grown adults who haven't been in church since childhood—or have never been in church.

THE THIRD VALUE: GET IN TOUCH WITH OUR INNER "REVOLUTIONARY"

It may sound offbeat, but the third value that we stumbled on was *getting in touch with our inner revolutionary*. Again I am not speaking of terrorist tactics that destroy human life but their ability to recruit people to a cause. Instead of shouting, "We have a new thing!" out front, we discovered that it is more effective to look around the edges for disenfranchised, even dissatisfied people. As I have mentioned, every church seems to have a group of "holy dissatisfied" folks. They aren't troublemakers; they just have a sense that God is up to something so much greater than they are seeing in the local church.

These people are marked by three characteristics:

- A positive hope that there is something more, even though the church is not reaching what they feel is its potential,

- Already serving in activities outside the formal church structure,

- Ample relationships outside the church, especially with people who don't share their faith journey.

These folks didn't respond to announcements and promotions but to conversations about what was happening around the world and a question, "Could this happen here?" Whereas a typical program couldn't intrigue them, the simplicity of the DMM strategy infused them with courage and confidence that they could do this.

These conversations led to many mini-training sessions about how to lead a discovery group, followed by many counterintuitive principles that allow movements to happen. *Mini*-training sessions helped us understand the need for *many* training sessions. While surveying movement leaders around the world we found that six formal trainings were necessary for the DNA of the movement to leak deep enough into people to make them effective disciple-making disciples.

Shock came when we began implementing these groups. More than half of them failed!

THE FOURTH VALUE: ACCEPT FAILURE AS THE PATH TO SUCCESS

And we soon came upon our fourth value: *failure is the path to success*. That might be a great line in a speech, but it is not a pleasantly accepted practice in America. No one likes to fail!

You won't find conferences that highlight failure—only success. When people inquire about our success with this strategy, they are always interested in how many groups, how many generations, how much success, and so forth.

One late insight into the path to success through failure was learned well after we took the plunge. All the movements that caught our attention and convinced us to move in this direction had an underground, as well as aboveground, story. Most people tell the aboveground story.

Using the analogy of a building, there is sufficient work done out of sight that ensures the structure is built on a good foundation and will stand the test of time. Let me say this again, *most movements tell the aboveground story* describing the aboveground structure as it currently exists. You have to dig to get the story of the below-ground activity.

I learned a valuable lesson early in my relationship with Willow Creek. One of their early technical staff was leading a seminar on lighting. There was a lot of insanely expensive lighting equipment in the room. He started the workshop by saying, "None of this was here when we started. We started by punching holes in coffee cans, sticking light bulbs though them and stringing extension cords dangerously between them." He went on to make the point that if you are going to listen to the "Willow" story, make sure you are talking to people who were there before all the bells and whistles. They will talk about the "whys" that drove them to use whatever they had. It is not the toys that make Willow he said, it is the values.

We discovered that even David Watson and Victor John had at least six years underground before seeing results. Cityteam[3] wandered in the wilderness as long as nine years before gaining traction. In fact, Dave Hunt of Cityteam told me that they had at least two restarts in all of the cities in the United States in which they are working.

Failure, as in groups starting and then having people drop out or find excuses not to attend, became an all too familiar reality. Group facilitators not understanding the criticality of the DNA was also common. People freewheeling their own designer strategies popped up all the time. This led to another key learning, which might seem like the "DUH!" of the decade but as obvious as it is, it remains critical. Not only did we learn that we needed to fail faster, but we also needed to fail smarter.

This realization eased the pain of failure. We took every opportunity to make each failure a learning experience. Connecting leaders to one another and providing tools for them to share their learning with one another helped establish a culture that was constantly in a beta-testing mode, so we could celebrate failure through learning. One of our first learning experiences came with the title of our small groups. Many of our partners around the world use DBS or "Discovery Bible Study" to describe their groups. While failing to start a group, one of our leaders helped us identify a problem with that phrase.

Upon asking friends to join a Discovery Bible Study group to read the Bible to find out what God says about life, they found resistance. Wanting to learn from our mistakes, we had them explore the rejections they had received and the reasons behind them. The answer was enlightening to say the least. The nonbelievers answered that a "Bible Study" was a place where Christians go to display their knowledge about the Bible. Since they knew nothing about the Bible, they didn't want to go to another place where they felt stupid. From then on we began calling our groups Discovery Groups rather than Discovery Bible Studies.

THE FIFTH VALUE: TRAIN, TRAIN, AND RETRAIN

Every moment has its own unique learnings, because it targets a unique culture. The idea of a one-size-fits-all strategy is simply misguided. So implementation and execution have to include many pivots based on the learnings. To ensure that all this learning was moving through our Go-side culture, we have a commitment to our fifth value: *train, train, and retrain*. Stan Parks says in an interview on the Disciple-Making Movements Sandbox that before we see Disciple-Making Movements in North America, we will have to see training movements. We now believe that wholeheartedly.

To care for and create this learning environment, we discovered that the casual exchange of learning was helpful but not sufficient. There was and is a need to catalog and categorize the learning. We had to develop the disciple to communicate it in formal settings. We discovered that allowing the give and take of Q & A could further infect our disciple-making disciples with the DNA of DMM. Many varied training opportunities are needed. We provide online training that our facilitators can take advantage of 24/7. We hold regular four-hour sessions to help encourage their skill building.

We have a Discover DMM seven-hour experience that give participants a chance to learn concepts and practice skills. We offer an eight-week follow up to Discover DMM to continue to leak the thinking into our disciple-makers. We have monthly gatherings of our Catalyst to talk about learnings. TTR-train, train and re-Train has become a mantra for us.

We use a flush-and-drip strategy. We begin with a four-hour immersion in the discovery process and movement thinking for our facilitators (the flush). Following this are many opportunities to hone their skills and mind-set (the drip).

This commitment to training grew not only out of our practitioners but also out of our leaders. We were learning both inside and outside of our movement efforts. We learned how to better put words to our instruction. We learned new metaphors to explain what we were up to and new exercises to help get ideas across. We learned from others how to train better.

THE SIXTH VALUE: CHALLENGE DUNNING-KRUGER DISEASE

Coaching and mentoring are not easy with suburbanite Americans, who neither seek nor especially appreciate it. A spirit of competence resides inside the suburban mentality that may arise from a sense of democracy or even insecurity, but it causes people to resist seeking advice and accepting evaluation from others. I would say that this idea might even be more intense in the modern Christian culture, especially when it comes to disciple-making.

Those who "sell" a Disciple-Making Movement strategy often overuse the world "simple." This leads to a conclusion by those hearing that it is "simplistic." And this is wrong on at least two accounts.

It isn't simple because you are dealing with a fixed Christian culture that is not welcoming to radical change. Too often methodologies are closely attached to theologies. The average modern

Christian views theology as fixed. If methodologies and theologies are connected then threatening one threatens the other. A change in methodology becomes a fight for orthodoxy.

Second, although using the principles of multiplicative disciple-making is simple, it is not easy. Some major "rethinking" or repro-gramming needs to be done before the average person can be effective. The more "trained" a person is, the more reprogramming has to be done.

Researchers David Dunning and Justin Kruger quantified this thought in establishing the Dunning-Kruger Effect.[4] They demon-strated that our greatest enemy is not what we know but what we don't know that we don't know. In fact they demonstrated that the less competent we are the more likely we are to make this mistake. They merely proved what Epictetus said, "It is impossible for a man to learn what he thinks he already knows."

Beware of the attitude, "I got this," because chances are they haven't! Observe, coach, and train with a vengeance. It helped our coaches get better by coaching and it improves the practice of disci-ple-making at the street level. Ultimately it moves the Great Com-mission toward completion.

On a practical level we offer short, end-of-the-workday, Happy Hour Coaching sessions where people could stop by on their way home and interact with one another. We committed to calling every new group facilitator weekly for the first six to eight weeks. We expected the group that they grew out of to provide coaching, but we also had some of our "super coaches" get in the game with them to discover how we could help newer facilitators.

Since this is not leading-edge but bleeding-edge stuff, it becomes vital to have a value of training, coaching, and mentoring at the heart of catalyzing a movement. Movements live and die on good

Movements live and die on good mentoring and coaching.

mentoring and coaching. So we started our movement catalyzing efforts surrounded with coaching opportunities. We can't let what people don't know that they don't know hinder them from becoming players in Jesus' kingdom work!

We have an evolving plan to meet the challenge of my dream turned into a nightmare turned into a strategy. Finally, we are beginning to see a readjustment to a whole new way of thinking about the Great Commission.

DISCOVERING
A JOURNEY

MAKING DISCIPLE-
MAKING DISCIPLES

In a 2005 TED talk, Terry Moore humorously and humbly suggested to one of the most educated, sophisticated, and culturally savvy audiences that they were taught to tie their shoes wrong. An audacious and seemly preposterous task for such an erudite audience. But if you listened and learned you discovered he was exactly right.

I finished the *Camino de Santiago* Pilgrimage in May 2014. When you're walking fifteen miles a day, having your shoestrings tied correctly is a significant issue. The way I had originally been taught to tie my shoes would mean retying them several times a day. But I listened, learned, and improved. Every day for thirty-one days, I tied my Northface Hedgehogs the way Terry taught me, and my shoestrings stayed tied.

I feel somewhat like Terry in this book. I am facing at least a thousand years of church history or better and suggesting that we may have been doing it wrong all this time. Well, let me be accurate. Terry suggested that the way most of us were taught to tie our shoes was not wrong but not the most efficient way. The way we've been promoting the teachings of Jesus may not be the most efficient, especially as the population of the earth moves toward ten billion.

Our new paradigms of

- everyone willing to obey Jesus is a disciple,
- teaching as causing people to learn,
- building obedience-focused platforms,
- radically eliminating dependency on humans,

allowed us to connect with the heart of what we saw happening overseas and get over our ethnocentric selves so it could happen here.

At Shoal Creek, we no longer teach people to share their faith. In the culture I live in people don't want to know what you believe or why you believe it. They don't want to be sold on a proposition; they are interested in your life. And if you learn to share your life rather than a set of facts that you believe in, they will engage.

For the longest time, I was trained to equip people to be sales reps for Jesus. Selling vacuum cleaners or selling Jesus—the techniques aren't all that different—the motivation, yes, but the techniques, no. From the first billboard to the Fuller Brush Man through the Avon Lady to the commercials on TV up to the ubiquitous advertising that sneaks onto every screen we own, we are an over-sold culture.

Mix our oversold psyche with the loss of trustable authority in our world and we have become islands of isolated skeptics inventing our own authority structures to empower a folk religion in each of us. Who then are you to tell me what to believe? What gives you the right to presume that I need changing?

Living in this culture and hoping to help others find Jesus has led us to challenge the techniques given to us by the historic church. The altar call, sinner's prayer, and even personal evangelism are all less than three hundred years old.

We discovered that people in our world were still interested in Jesus, God, and the Bible; just not in church, and especially not church people telling them they didn't believe in the right things. How could we get those who were never going to come to a Sunday morning service close to Jesus?

This led us to learn a simple, repeatable way of taking anyone into a discipling relationship and showing them how to connect with God through reading, obeying, and sharing the Bible. The process is simple enough that they can repeat it where they live, learn, work, or play. The self-replicating nature frees the gospel from the forms of church, missional communities, and discipleship programs and lets the gospel run free through social networks.

What does it look like? Seven basic questions make up the backbone of the discovery process.

1. How did you do on your "I will" and "sharing"? (This is asked after the first meeting)

2. What are you thankful for?

3. What is stressing you out today?

4. Do you have a need or does someone you know have a need that this group could meet?

5. What does God have to say today? (a passage of Scripture goes here)

6. If this is God speaking, what are you going to do about it? (usually stated as "I will . . .")

7. Who can you share with this week what God is doing in your life?

There is nothing outside the Bible to be read or discussed. Each week, participants proceed through a prescribed list of Bible passages. We developed this path around seven spiritual disciplines (The 7 Journeys) that are key to living a life of obedience to Jesus.

This slow methodical process gives opportunity for spiritual growth. Most people don't believe they are *lost*. To them that is a derogatory term. It takes time for them to read and hear from God. As they move through the Bible, they discover for themselves that humankind has rebelled. They see firsthand what God is up to in this world. He tells them what His values are. The facilitators are along for the ride as witnesses. My job is to be a witness of God's work in me and to let Him be the teacher and draw people to Himself (see John 6:44–46).

DISCOVERY VERSUS JOURNEY

The groups we ask people to join have two different names in our hybrid structure. On the Come-side, they are called Journey Groups; and on the Go-side, they are referred to as Discovery Groups. Journey Groups work on a semester basis. They start three times a year with a formal recruitment process both for members and facilitators. The names we use for different groups are inconsequential to the process and chosen for utilitarian reasons only.

Because of the nature of our Sunday service (no musical worship, although we do listen to music), we don't attract many Christians. What we learned from David Watson, coauthor of *Contagious Disciple-Making*, was our appeal to "persons of peace." Find this concept in Luke 10, where Jesus is training his disciples. He tells them to find a home where there is receptivity to the gospel and stay there. This home would represent a "person or house of peace."

Each month, about forty families visit our services. Fifty percent of those self-identify as nonbelievers. These folks are potential "persons of peace." Our Journey Groups are designed to disciple them into a relationship with the Creator who wants to be their Father.

When people ask, "What is a Journey Group?" our response is that it is a place to make some friends, learn to read the Bible, and hear what God has to say about life. We've been told what to think and believe for too long; now it is God's turn to speak, and that's what happens at a Journey Group.

Let me explain briefly the difference between Journey and Discovery Groups. When you are inside them there is no difference. We use the same seven questions and the same list of Bible passages. The difference is in how they start.

Journey Groups have an artificial start to them. We engineer starts three times a year. Discovery Groups are more organic. They start where people live, learn, work, and play. They may start out of a Journey Group, but there is no prescribed start to a Discovery Group.

For instance as someone in a Journey Group is sharing with a friend what God is up to in his life, the friend may ask where he is learning all this spiritual stuff. It would be natural then to invite this friend to the Journey or Discovery Group. But our group facilitators are taught to think in terms of multiplication instead of growth. Instead of allowing the group to grow, the facilitator offers to help this group member start a group with a friend. This new group would be called a Discovery Group for our purposes, but the new group facilitator and group members may not even have a name for it.

The two names arise from our attempt to track generational growth, when groups birth groups or disciples make disciples. The two names help us facilitate where the gospel is moving in our community institutionally and organically. The training and facilitation for each type of group are exactly the same.

An invitation to a Journey Group can come from a friend or a promotional message from Shoal Creek. A Discovery Group is populated solely by personal invitation. Everyone in a Discovery Group will usually be a part of an existing network of friends. It might be a work or neighborhood network, but each of those attending will usually have a preexisting relationship.

The invitation for this group is simple. The spiritual catalyst for the group asks, "I am starting a group that is going to read the Bible together and discover what God has to say about life. Would you like to join us?" It is important that the invitee know that there is not going to be a subject-matter expert in the group. The group is going to do this together. They aren't going to be sharing their spiritual preferences or what they were taught as a kid. They are going to read the Bible and let God tell them in His own words what He says about life.

The fact that they will be doing this together will take the leadership spotlight off the spiritual catalyst pulling this together and begin to lessen the group members' dependence. It also sets up the potential to share the facilitation within the group. This in turn sets up the potential for this group to experience reproduction.

The vision for groups is not to build community, grow relationally, and build a tribe to do life with. Both Discovery Group and Journey Group facilitators are taught to think about generational growth. This means eliminating any unnecessary and often unseen dependencies that might arise.

THINKING DIFFERENTLY ABOUT FACILITATION

Each January, May, and September we seek facilitators for these groups. We require facilitators to do four things:

1. Attend a four-hour training session on how to use the discovery process.

2. Follow the prescribed process by asking all seven questions each group meeting.

3. Use the list of passages that we provide.

4. Respond to their assigned coach when he or she calls.

We commission both doubters and worshipers to facilitate these groups. Our comfort level comes from two places. One, Jesus showed no anxiety when He commissioned both groups to take His mission forward. And two, we make the Bible the authority in these groups, so we aren't leader dependent.

Our facilitator training provides the vision for the group. These groups are designed to learn to read the Bible and hear from God what He says about life. A group is not there to hear each other's opinions or the latest spiel from the latest spiritual guru or new-age diva. This is God's chance to speak directly to group members through reading, obeying, and sharing what He has written in the Bible.

Facilitators are equipped to ask the question, "Where does it say that *in this passage?*" This works for the person who likes to reference Oprah, Dr. Phil, Joel Osteen, or the latest Rick Warren book. It also works for the churched person who can't stay in one passage but has to bounce all around the Bible when answering questions.

We have discovered that when you have people who are inexperienced in the Bible, staying in one simple passage makes their initial experiences comfortable rather than making them feel dumb. When a flurry of Bible passages starts being tossed around, they shrink from the discussion and try to find a place to hide. The tragedy is they may never come back. So "Where does it say that in this passage?" is a key training point. To combat those who resist staying in the focal passage, the facilitator is to say, "Today we are trying to figure out what God is saying in this passage. We will talk about the other passages when the group is finished."

We also want our facilitators to understand that this is a process of discovery. People buy into, believe, and act on their own conclusions far more than the conclusions given to them by other people. The group is designed for people to hear from God themselves, so the idea of teaching or telling people what to believe about the passage doesn't belong in a Journey (or Discovery) Group.

It doesn't take a doctoral dissertation to prove that as humans we love to figure things out for ourselves. My oldest daughter was fond of a phrase that drilled this truth into me. From the time she could put sentences together, when I would try to help her with anything, she would look at me and say, "By myself!" When we are intimately acquainted with all the twists and turns of our own thinking, we have an organic attachment to the conclusions of our mental activity.

The success of facilitators is determined not by how much but how little they talk or persuade. Training facilitators to focus on asking more questions than giving answers helps them see their critical role in the discovery of God's truth. Learning starts when we realize that we can stop trying to tell people what to believe and start suggesting what they should be thinking about trusting in.

> **Success of facilitators is determined not by how much but how little they talk or persuade.**

Many facilitators have the gift of hospitality and love having people in their homes. They may unintentionally hinder the flow of the generational growth of the gospel with this gift. If every person in a group is to be seen as a potential disciple-maker, facilitators must not do anything that others think they can't do.

Maybe the facilitator has a nice house, and not all the group attendees can see a group happening in their houses. Maybe the house is spotless or the hostess makes incredible treats for the group. For this reason, facilitators are trained to move Journey Group meetings around. Discovery Groups are encouraged to start on the turf of the spiritually interested or at least on neutral ground.

Another important shift is shared facilitation. If one facilitator is still doing all the facilitation after the third group meeting, he or she is doing a bad job! The process is so simple and repeatable that after being in a Journey/Discovery Group a few times, it is simple to ask the seven basic question and bring the accountability piece to the table. So, in effect, our facilitators are facilitator coaches.

This expectation can be laid out at the first meeting of Journey Groups; Discovery Groups may take a little more finesse. If a facilitator does a good job, he or she will have modeled for the members how easy facilitating is and be able to pass it on easily.

Dependency is a subtle and evil issue. The hard truth is that many of us love spiritual leadership because of the dependencies that it creates. Often others' dependency on us gives us purpose and meaning. It can even provide a diversion from our own pain as we help others deal with theirs. In the guise of wanting to follow Jesus, we inherently stunt people's growth by teaching them to depend on us, and we create unnecessary stress on ourselves.

It reminds me of a hard truth from Ben Franklin:

> I am for doing good to the poor, but I differ in opinion of the means. I think the best way of doing good to the poor, is not making them easy *in* poverty, but leading or driving them out of it. In my youth I travelled much, and I observed in different countries, that the more public provisions were made for the poor, the less they provided for themselves and of course became poorer. And, on the contrary, the less was done for them, the more they did for themselves, and became richer.[1]

This is true in the spiritual world as well. The more we do for people the worse off they are. It is no wonder we have a lethargic church in the West. Most of what flies under the name of ministry is a subtle codependent relationship between leaders and followers: leaders who need to be needed and followers who want someone besides themselves to be responsible for their spiritual journey.

Facilitators are coached to be catalytic so that their greatest joy is watching things move away from them. Generational growth is more deeply satisfying than any other spiritual emotion. As a grandfather of eight and counting there is no greater joy than watching your children raise children. It gets to the essence of the Great Commission as we teach people to be disciple-making disciples.

GROUP PROCESS

The process for facilitating a Journey/Discovery Group is simple by design (see appendix A: Facilitation Guide).

Since the members of a Discovery Group have preexisting relationships, you can jump right into the questions. The seven questions (see p. 123) represent biblical DNA, the genetic code of the spiritual life that Jesus left behind. The questions are the method by which the Spirit will transfer the genetic code into the lives of those being discipled.

Asking the question, "What are you thankful for?" gives the group an easy way to get started, and everyone can come up with something to say, even the introverts. You might notice that we don't start with prayer. Christians start groups with prayer; those who are far from God don't.

Often in a group of pre-Christians, once the group is going, someone might say, "Aren't we supposed to pray before we start?" The facilitator might say, "Would you like to pray?" Usually the response will be, "I don't know how to pray!"

This becomes a perfect learning moment. The facilitator can express that prayer can be as simple as telling God what we are thankful for. She or he can then point out what the group has been sharing that they are thankful for and that prayer is just telling God the same thing. The facilitator can just start the group over and say, "Let's tell God what we are thankful for."

The facilitator may then bow her head and listen as the group talks to God, but nothing in the Bible tells us to do that. So by bowing her head and closing her eyes, the facilitator is teaching the group that this is the proper way to pray. Disciples do what you do, not what you say! The group members will learn to pray as they answer the first two questions in a very natural and organic way.

As a facilitator, you must remember that you are also a group member. Your answers to the question will be a model for the group. Being thoughtful about your answers is important. Show other group members what thankfulness is by the honesty and transparency in your answers. One week, your answer to the question might be about your spouse serving you in some way. The next week, it might be about knowing that you live in the favor of your Father in heaven even though you screwed up at work.

Another key point—don't always go first or last. Vary how and when you answer the question so that you don't inadvertently teach your group that there is a right and wrong way for the facilitator to answer.

IS ORDER IMPORTANT?

Even though the first question is an easy ice-breaker and even the second, the questions don't have to go in the order listed. For instance, you can start with accountability. Asking how they did on their "I wills" and sharing from the previous week can be the first thing. Be patient with your group as they grow into learning to obey what God says. It will take some time for them to figure this out, but your consistent example will provide a beacon of light to them.

The third question—"What is stressing you out today?"—can be a time bomb. Asking a North American this can lead to a 30-minute answer. This is not a support group, so answers shouldn't be long and drawn out. This is one time when it may be beneficial for you to answer the question first, providing a model for how it should be done. Remember that a Discovery Group is made up of people who have a preexisting relationship, so this is not their only connection. Because of this connection, they have plenty of time to talk about life outside the group.

Occasionally, a group member will have an issue that requires the facilitator to put aside the passage from the Bible. In these moments, it is appropriate to be transparent and take the pressure of getting to the passage off the group. If this happens too frequently, you probably have a group member whose motivation to be in the group is not to hear from God but to gain a hearing for his or her problems.

This issue can kill a group, if it is not dealt with. Often you can simply suggest to the group that since they have had a hard time finishing each week everyone should try limiting their answers to each question to no more than two minutes. A humorous way to do this is to suggest that people share in sentences not paragraphs.

Group size can be an issue here as well.

If one person regularly takes up too much time, you may need to speak personally with that person and ask for help in keeping the group on task by shortening answers. Another way is to pass off the facilitation to the person who is the repeat offender. The Facilitators Guide offers some time guidelines. Give one of these to a new facilitator to emphasize the time-management issue.

Group size can be an issue here as well. Think of it this way: You have seven questions, and each question may average two minutes to answer. Simple math helps me see that I have fourteen minutes for each person. Multiply fourteen times the number of people in the group and now you have the challenge. If the group has six members, you'll need between one and a half and two hours for the meeting. So group size should be limited to five and under, at least for those being held in the United States. As an African friend once reminded me, "Americans wear their god on the wrist." Time is our greatest foe in the challenge to get people face-to-face with God.

The fourth question "Do you have a need or does anyone you know have a need that this group could meet?" is one of the hardest pieces of the DNA to get set. The question is meant to begin the

discipling process by involving group members in the second half of
the Great Commandment, loving others.

In the United States, *need* is often identified with money, so the
question is skewed in people's mind toward poverty. It takes time to
help people have eyes for others in their immediate context. Often,
you as the facilitator can find a need in the neighborhood or workplace that can be met. Maybe someone is undergoing chemo and
needs meals, housework, or help getting kids to school.

Serving together changing the world around you gets a group
into the flow of what God is all about. It imprints in group members
that a relationship with God is lived out, not just thought about.
It is vital to wrestle this question to reality in a group. This, along
with the sixth question, in which everyone flushes out their "I will"
statements, are the bookends of the obedience-focused culture in a
Journey/Discovery Group.

READING THE BIBLE TOGETHER

The fifth question provides the opportunity for the group to open
the Bible and hear directly from God. Often group members will
not have Bibles, or someone will have a translation of the Bible that
is difficult to understand. For the first couple of meetings, it may be
best for you to print off copies of the passage. You may also find
yourself in the Bible sales consultant mode, which is a good thing.
Group members having a readable Bible that they own would be a
significant goal early in the group process.

We encourage our facilitators to print two copies of two different modern translations of the Bible or bring two different versions
of the Bible with you. Not only does this solve the issue of someone
in your group not having a Bible, but it also allows time to explain
how the Bible is laid out. Before discovering this, we exposed an
assumption about Bible familiarity that was almost fatal in a group.

A group member was asked to read 1 John 5:13. When he began, reading many in the group began to screw up their faces and wonder what version he was reading out of. The facilitator stopped him and asked him to check to make sure that he was in "First" John. He proudly held up his Bible and said, "I turned to the first John and found chapter 5 verse 13."

For those of us familiar with the Bible, we know that he was in the Gospel According to John not the First Epistle of John. Most people aren't familiar with the organization of the Bible, so just turning to passages in the Bible can be cause undue anxiety. Having sheets with Bible verses printed on paper gives you a chance to explain how the Bible is organized. Once group members have Bibles of their own, practice finding something familiar like John 3:16 to create more comfort in getting around the Bible.

Showing members the contents page in front of the Bible gives them a tool to start with. Explaining the difference between a book, a chapter, and a verse equips them to get around in the Bible on their own. Practicing finding passages they may have heard of, such as John 3:16 and Psalm 23, gives them confidence that they won't be put in a situation of feeling stupid if they have to find a location in the Bible.

Tell the group that you are going to read the passage twice. If it is a long passage (more than ten verses), break the passage into chunks of five verses and have them pass the sheet around and share the reading. You can alternately highlight five verses on the sheet with Bible verses on it with a colored highlighter to make it easier for them to keep track as they pass the sheet around.

Make sure as you share the instructions that you also let them know that if they are uncomfortable reading out loud to just keep passing the paper on. There is no need to let someone's literacy skills get in the way of them connecting with God.

When you prepare your printed sheets, or if you bring two Bibles, it is good to have two different versions of the Bible available.

The passage is going to be read twice, so they get two chances to hear it with slightly different wording. Although Eugene Peterson's *The Message* is a great Bible to have for a person not familiar with the Bible, it is not a good choice for one of your versions. The step after reading the passage twice is to have someone in the group retell the passage in his or her own words. Unfortunately, Eugene Peterson is so eloquent that once his paraphrase is read, there is very little improvement to find. Using *The Message* can shut down the discussion quickly because no one can add anything to what Peterson has written.

When choosing a version of the Bible to use make sure that it is a modern translation. Even the King James Bible has been updated. The New King James (NKJV) or the New International Readers Version (NIRV) are great versions to choose from. The Voice is a new version of the Bible that is an excellent choice as well as the New English Bible (NET). You'll find that many people will find resources like YouVersion and Biblegateway.com before they will own a Bible. It is not unusual for them to read from their phones or iPads.

GIVE THEM A HEADS UP!

Before reading the passage, ask someone in the group to listen closely so she can start putting the passage in her own words. This gives the person a chance to listen closely rather than be surprised by the assignment at the end of the reading. *NOTE: If you haven't gotten the message so far, you want to do everything to avoid making people feel "less than."*

Once the person assigned to put the passage into his own words seems to be struggling or finished, ask the entire group to help. This can create a robust discussion around a passage. You want them to get the core or central truth from the passage. For instance, if you are in Genesis 1, the point is not creation versus evolution but that God is the Creator of all there is. Don't get sidetracked on peripheral issues.

As you become accustomed to facilitating the group, you may find the following sets of questions helpful to stimulate discussion around the key points. These aren't necessary if your group is relating to the passage and circling around the main points in the passage.

These three questions are aimed at getting personal responses to the passage:

- What grabbed your attention?

- What did you like in the passage?

- What bothered you in the passage?

These three are focused on God's intention in communicating to us:

- What does this say about God?

- What does this say about mankind?

- What does this say about the life God wants us to live?

While pursuing a graduate degree in theology, I learned to memorize long lists of theological minutia using acronyms. That skill—affectionately called Budak-ing—might help you remember these two sets of questions. Take the first letter of each word and make a sentence out of them. For example, "A Lemon Bite Gathers Many Looks." Notice the A, L, B, G, M, and L. They refer to *attention, like, bother, God, mankind,* and *life.* The phrase comes from my oldest son using his niece as a guinea pig in a restaurant by offering her the lemon out of his iced tea when she was small. Every time she took it and bit into it, she shuddered. The entire restaurant would look and laugh—a lemon bite gathers many looks.

If you need help stimulating discussion, then remember that A (attention) Lemon (like) Bite (bothers) Gathers (God) Many (mankind) Looks (life). It may sound corny, but I have a graduate degree in theology because of that skill. Unfortunately, it may mean I am highly educated to be utterly useless!

GETTING TO "I WILL . . ."

The last set of questions, "What does this passage say about God, mankind, and the life that He wants us to live?" can set up the sixth piece of the DNA very easily. It makes the transition to an "I will" statement very natural.

The sixth question asks, "If this is God speaking, what are you going to do about it?" It is easy to state this as "I will. . . ." As time goes on, your group will begin to refer to this as their "I wills."

At first, it is often hard for people to come up with tangible, actionable activities. Since the SMART acronym is so prevalent in the business culture, it is natural to suggest that their "I wills" be Specific, Measurable, Achievable, Realistic, and Time-bound. Another way to say it is, "In the next twenty-four to forty-eight hours, what can you do in response to what God is saying here?"

The "I will" statements to be acted upon have to be specific. One way to test them is to ask, "So when you come back next week, how will we know whether you've done that 'I will' or not?" This helps your group members clarify how it is they want to respond to God.

Be patient, have grace, and provide a good model as your group gets used to acting on the truth found in the Bible. While studying Genesis 1, it is not unusual to find people wanting to start recycling to show God they care for His creation. That is a tangible way of responding to the truth. Simple acts of response to God speaking is our goal.

Watch for trends in your group, such as people not doing their "I wills." This probably is a sign of their spiritual temperature. Since you don't want to spin your wheels, be ready to ask them after three or four weeks how you can help them follow through on their "I wills."

Usually this kind of attention will either energize someone's spiritual interest or expose that there is no spiritual appetite there.

Another trend is to have the same "I will" statement every week. Obviously, we could all focus on a few things for a long time and grow through that focus. But repeating an "I will" can expose spiritual laziness and perpetuate our attempts to plant good seed in infertile soil. Simply say, "Uh-oh, you had that 'I will' last week, you are going to need to find another this week"; or "This is a different passage, I think we might need a different 'I will'." This will communicate to the group that they need to be a bit more creative in listening to what God is saying. If need be, have the group help someone develop an "I will." Remember this group already has preexisting relationships, so their knowledge about one another's lives is plentiful. Above all, don't hesitate to provide a constant, gentle accountability toward obeying what God says. That was Jesus' command: "teach them to obey all that I have commanded you."

REPLICATION

The seventh question, "Who can you share with this week what God is doing in your life?" brings the DNA of replication to the process.

Each group member is asked to name someone to share with in the coming week. The content of the sharing can be related to what they are reading and obeying from the Bible or in general what God is doing in his or her life.

As early as possible in the discipling process, the disciple is taught to identify with Jesus. This is not done in obnoxious ways that drive up walls between friends or relatives, but in simple, obvious ways. Sharing should not be persuasive. People feel the pressure of persuasion and react by putting up barriers and boundaries to a relationship, but an experience or a story draws them in. When someone shares what is going on in his life, we listen, draw close, and enjoy the invitation to another's internal world.

Recently a man who had never read the Bible before shared that reading the Bible helped him sleep at night. He hadn't slept well for months due to a relationship that was on the rocks. He began reading the Bible and sleeping. So he shared with friends that the Bible was allowing him to sleep at night. This is real, related, and very provocative!

We listen, draw close, and enjoy the invitation to another's internal world.

Experienced Christians have the hardest time with this because their ability to share their lives has been shaped by a world that values inauthenticity. We have been taught that it is important to be buttoned down and have your act together in the Christian world. Training churched folk to be natural in sharing their stories is a little like training a cat to shake hands and roll over. It is not impossible, but if you accomplish the task you have the Midas touch.

Group members often share by mentioning to friends that they learned something while reading the Bible. Since these group members are coming from pre-Christian relational networks, this mention creates a conversation, one that can lead to replication. When friends learn that someone is in a group reading the Bible, and no one is shoving religion down their throats, it piques their interest. Some might even want to join the group. This is where the DNA of replication begins. Groups need to multiply, not grow.

The Bible is the authority in the discovery process, so no need exists for a subject-matter expert to explain it to people. God's Word is not being taught, but read and obeyed. God is the teacher leading people to Jesus (John 6:44–46). The simple, repeatable discovery process allows the group to multiply. Everyone in the first group has seen the simple seven questions asked, and they have probably taken a turn at facilitating.

When a friend asks to join, a facilitator can suggest that, instead of adding to this group, which will further create time issues, start another group. This is a winnable argument, because the process is so easy anyone can do it. Just do what has been done in the initial group.

The initial group facilitator can regularly coach the group member as she or he begins this new group. Regular phone calls or personal meetings to talk through the rough spots and issues that develop will increase the new facilitator's confidence. Since the leadership development is built-in rather than bolted on, every group member is equipped to start a group.

QUESTIONS OF TIME

Finally, the group wraps up by reviewing any decisions that were made when discussing the question about needs that could be met. Be sure not to dismiss before reviewing the next meeting time to make sure everyone is clear when and where the next gathering is, especially if you are moving the venue around to different homes or apartments. At this point, the group is finished. It is not unusual for the group discussion to continue informally. Members will leave at their leisure.

The process described above assumes no artificial constraints. If a Discovery Group is happening over a lunch hour in the workplace, it is difficult to get more than three or four people through this process in a meaningful fashion.

Here are some strategies to alleviate the time pressure:

ELECTRONIC COMMUNICATION

The first three questions can be asked and answered via e-mail, text, or chat the morning of the group. This allows the group to start with reading the passage and jump right in when they are together.

THREE-COLUMN METHOD

The title of this method comes from the practice of turning a sheet of paper to a landscape format and dividing the sheet into three columns. This is not necessary but can be useful. The columns refer to three separate steps in this process (see sample in appendix B). Group members get the passage the previous week and complete the three-column study prior to the next meeting.

In the first column, the passage is copied word for word from the Bible. In a digital world, many people recoil at this. Why not cut and paste? The exercise of copying by hand from the Bible is a way to read slower than you normally do. Word by word the Bible is moved from the page in the Bible to a page in a notebook or journal.

This slow word-for-word process allows the brain to see the Bible passage up close and feel the passage in a way that you can't any other way. It may be difficult to get people to pull out a writing utensil and do this, but once they do they will be astounded by the depth of the experience.

After copying the passage from their Bible to their notebook or journal, the second step or column asks them to put the passage in their own words. This process causes decisions to be made about what God is trying to say in this passage. When it becomes time, several group members can read aloud what they wrote down in the second column, so it accomplishes the fifth question in the discovery process. Group members don't have to hurry through this Bible portion, since they have spent time personally in this passage before the meeting.

The second column will be a challenge to those who don't like to write or express themselves in writing. Encouraging perseverance will reap valuable rewards. The slow process of copying and rewording the passage brings us as close to the mind of God as we can ever get in this world.

The third column or step has two separate activities. If the note-book or journal is turned to landscape, then divide this column into a top half and a bottom half. On the top half, write down the "I will" statement. On the bottom half, write down the answer to the "share" question.

This process can be accomplished by group members before they arrive. The group can move into the first three questions and the Bible discussion portion of the group is shortened

The Three-Column Study accomplishes two key objectives: get-ting people up close and personal with the Bible and creating effec-tive use of time when there is a limited amount of time available.

The discovery process, whether accomplished in a group format or by using the Three-Column method, gets people into the Bible. There is no traction in the spiritual journey without getting your fingerprints on the Bible. Both of these tools allow people to dis-cover how they can relate to God personally. They are equipped to make disciple-making disciples because they can easily pass this on to friends, relatives, and workmates.

THE 7 JOURNEYS

MOVING FROM ANALOG TO DIGITAL SPIRITUALITY

After hours of listening to David Watson, coauthor of *Contagious Disciple-Making*, train in many different contexts, we discovered that the DNA he communicates in discovery-based, obedience-focused disciple-making meshes with the DNA at Shoal Creek, especially with our paradigm of the spiritual life—the 7 Journeys:

1. Earner to Heir—Trust

2. Self-Hearted to Soft-Hearted—Obey

3. Receiver to Giver—Share

4. Isolation to Community—Relate

5. Consumer to Producer—Serve

6. Charitable to Extravagant—Give

7. Traveler to Guide—Disciple

Instead of starting with traditional evangelism, we begin by showing people how they can invite their friends, neighbors, and workmates to participate in a group that reads the Bible together and discovers what God has to say about life. In effect they start to make disciple-making disciples of pre-Christians. This idea is actually not as novel as one might think, for it has already produced millions of followers of Christ in the East and to date has caused at least forty thousand churches to form (see Bhojpuri story in chap. 5).

TRADITIONAL EVANGELISM

Traditional practice has been for believers to share their faith with pre-Christians and/or maybe invite them to a church meeting. Through a linear process, someone would accept Jesus as their Savior and begin regular church attendance. They in turn would be taught to share their faith. Usually this entails learning enough information to answer all the common questions asked about Christianity so that people feel comfortable attempting to convince someone to believe in Jesus.

This process is widely promoted, yet seldom practiced. Studies continually show that although Christians believe they should share their faith less than half of them do. James Kennedy, founder of Evangelism Explosion, is often quoted as saying that 95 percent of Christians today have never led a person to Christ. I am not sure that he had George Barna[1] to back him on that statistic, but it wouldn't be hard to substantiate in the average church.

Rather than perpetuate a failing system of propagating the faith, we follow a new approach at Shoal Creek, one learned from the Bhojpuri in India and repeated in many other cultures. It's a strategy that creates opportunities for people to read, obey, and share what God is teaching them through the Bible. This simple, repeatable process allows anyone, regardless of personality and giftedness, to make disciple-making disciples. Instead of inviting friends to church so someone else can tell them about Jesus, people in our fellowship invite friends to read the Bible with them and discover what God has to say about life.

The groups gather around the Bible as the authority, endeavor to do what God says, and then share it with their friends. In the context of obedience-focused groups, friends, neighbors, and workmates discover together without a subject-matter expert present. John 6:45—"Among the prophets, it's written, 'Everyone will be taught of God.' So everyone who has heard and learned from the Father finds Me."—becomes a reality as God is the teacher and leads people to His Son. The amazing power of starting people on a God-dependent spiritual journey rather than one that relies on an individual or institution provides the platform for a culture that replicates.

The 7 Journeys provides a paradigm for the spiritual pilgrimage that accounts for both the reality of individual experience and the truth God has given us. It departs from current spiritual life teaching by providing for a lifelong experience in all of God's truth rather than proceeding through steps, stages, or levels. Synergy occurs between how someone begins to follow Jesus and the path they follow through life.

At Shoal Creek, we've found this extremely helpful in working with people who are seeking to understand more about God, Jesus, and the Bible. Instead of emphasizing fixed growth points, the 7 Journeys focuses on movement. It allows people to mature without implying they have mastered an area and to regress without giving up on the journey.

The concept of movement also engages reality. Take, for instance, the first journey of moving from earner to heir. Despite how you define a person entering into the family of God, either by a gradual process or a sudden event, everyone has a lifelong journey of discovering that the earner mentality is embedded in their flesh. No matter the distance from a point of conversion or the amount of knowledge they possess, it takes a lifetime to eradicate that earner mentality.

Pre-Christians need navigational aids. It is important to share a map that outlines the journey and a compass that points in the right directions as they discover where they are on their personal maps.

Contrary to popular evangelical approaches which invite people to explore a relationship with God, everyone has a relationship with God. We often fail to understand that everyone already has a Creator/Creature relationship. They enjoy the creation that He has made and often give thanks for what they perceive to be blessings from their Creator. Our language must acknowledge this and not deny the very theology we espouse: He created everything and everyone.

When we offer to help people develop a relationship with God, it causes a disconnect from the start. They feel as if they have a relationship and the Bible declares they do, He is their Creator.

Too often, we refer to a "personal relationship" with God when, in fact, what we're talking about is a prescribed path of knowledge or assent to a set of facts that rarely sets someone up to have an intimate relationship with a father in heaven.

Our work is to deepen people's relationship with God. Beginning to read the Bible for themselves helps them move from a Creator/Creature relationship to a Father/Child relationship. We hope to help them see that their Creator wants to be their Father and has wisdom about life in this world and the world to come that will allow them to live in His family now and forever.

THE NATURE OF THE 7 JOURNEYS

The concept of the nonlinear nature of the 7 Journeys arose out of yearly visits to Disney World. My in-laws lived about 80 miles from Disney in Florida. Every year when we visited, my father-in-law thought it was his duty to treat us to Walt's place, so we took the obligatory trip from Venice to Orlando to visit Mickey's world.

After several visits, I became enthralled with the map of the theme park, so enthralled that I memorized it and could make pretty efficient decisions without referring to it. When leaving Tomorrow-land, we didn't have to go through Fantasyland to get to Frontier-land. We could go straight from Tomorrowland to Frontierland. Direct connections from each of the "lands" to the others meant we could visit lands in whatever order we chose (following a digital map); we didn't have to go around the park in a particu-lar order (following the analog map).

> **The synergy and interactions among different areas weren't apparent.**

At this time, I was also engaged in rethinking a schematic of the spiritual life. Here, too, I was messing with thoughts of digital versus analog, sequential versus random, and linear versus circu-lar. The old paradigms or schematics—Navigator Wheel, Bill Bright's 10 Basic Steps, Willow Creek's 5 Gs, even Rick Warren's baseball diamond—caused serious problems for me. They had a rather linear feel to them. The steps or next levels had the feel of leaving the others areas behind, rewarding spiritual maturity with badges or certifications. They seemed to be based on an educational model of competency achievement in levels.

I wanted to revisit certain fundamental truths regularly, but they were encased in the beginning levels of these paradigms. The mental models I grew up with indicated that I was regressing in my journey in any attempt to explore what a "cross-centered" life was.

Another discomfort related to the areas as parts of the whole, pieces of an interlocking puzzle yet separate. The synergy and interactions among different areas weren't apparent in these highly compartmentalized schematics. My understanding of my position in God's family directly relates to how I am able to serve God using the resources He has given to me. I longed to have fewer boundaries and more synergy among the keys areas of the spiritual journey.

Others' schematics also seemed couched in the Greek mind-set—dependent on gaining knowledge rather than on driving toward an intimate emotional relationship with a Creator God. I needed something that not only addressed my mind but also exposed me to a more emotional and less cognitive approach to the spiritual life.

Through a series of real-life field tests, the 7 Journeys came into existence. Each journey is defined as a movement from one extreme to another. This indicates that we never complete the journey this side of the grave. Each journey is also defined by a verb. Moving from earner to heir in our relationship with God requires that we stop trusting in ourselves and our efforts to please God and begin to trust in who He is and that what He has done is sufficient for our place in His family.

The journeys resemble the map at Disney World. You can move from one to the other directly. As the Spirit teaches and moves in your life, you can flow from one to the other. They are digital (CD) rather than analog (cassette tape). You don't have to go through all the songs to get to the one you want. You simply go right to it. So, too, with the Spirit, which, interacting with us, can move freely from one arena to another.

THREE KEY UNDERSTANDINGS

There are three key understandings about the journeys that help to engage them. First, what we think is good or right can actually be disruptive to our spiritual growth. God's plans for our lives are often counterintuitive to what we think or feel. Following Him can be both exciting and confusing as we soon realize we don't know what is best even for ourselves and trust that He does. The analogy of a fish feeling wet used in a previous chapter is appropriate here. What

Each journey is defined as a movement from one extreme to another.

works for us in life, our style of relating, becomes natural, but doesn't always jive with God's wisdom for life as we will soon see.

Second—and there is no easy way to put this—we are worse off than we think, but we are more loved than we could ever imagine. The Bible declares we have all compiled a long history of living apart from God. Yet it also points out how much God loves us, so much so that He sent His only Son to die in our place. Crazy, huh?

I like to think of this as the chemistry of grace, the connection between our being made in the image of God—our dignity—and our refusal to allow God to be the organizing principle of our lives— our depravity. As the two of those collide, the catalyst of God's unthinkable love for us makes for a life of transforming move through brokenness, repentance, abandonment, confidence, and release.

Third, we won't grow as fast as we desire. There is nothing instant about the spiritual journeys. There may be sudden leaps forward, but they are not the norm. The daily habits of living in obedience to God will transform from the inside out. It may take years to see the results, and they are often felt before they are seen.

However, we will grow as we partner with God and exercise our trust by regularly reading and obeying His Word. With Paul, often our weaknesses become a chance for God to declare His strength, and once again we experience the counterintuitive nature of this journey (2 Cor. 12:9). You see, becoming a fully devoted follower of Christ takes time. A lifetime actually!

WE ARE ALL THEOLOGIANS

Every human is a theologian. Most would deny it, but being a theologian is simply coming up with a workable strategy to deal with reality. There usually is a god, something that everything centers on. It provides the organizing principle for life. This god or organizing principle can be immoral or illegal, or it can be moral and welcomed by society. We often think of sexual encounters, illicit drug use, abuse of alcohol, or endless pursuit of material possessions as the key elements that would fill the spot reserved for God. However, family, serving, shopping, image management, and a host of other activities can also take God's place.

Being born into the world, we humans, made in the image of God, seek to figure life out. As we do this, we develop a personal style of relating to those around us. If your parents have high standards for behavior, education, and work, you might develop a penchant to please those around you. If your father or mother abandoned you early in life, you might develop a low sense of self, feel that you are not worth loving, and avoid deep connections.

Are we being formed according to the wisdom of God, Jesus, and the Bible; or formed out of our personal wisdom?

Putting those pieces of life together is what makes us theologians. Unfortunately that personal style of relating is not always informed by the Creator of life. The authority in our lives usually becomes an internal guidance system that flows from our figuring out how to navigate circumstances in the least painful way possible. Through our personal history, we develop a personal style of relating.

The thought that there is a Creator who might have something to say about what is going on inside of us occurs to few. Involving this Creator in the process of how I am formulating my responses to my external world, even while growing up under the influence of a Christian home, is rare. All the while, these internal processes are developing and maturing a theology or worldview that begins to serve my successful journey through life.

Dallas Willard reminds us that everyone is on a spiritual journey because we are spiritual people. The question is, what is the journey forming us into? Are we being formed according to the wisdom of God, Jesus, and the Bible; or formed out of our personal wisdom, our attempts to figure out how to painlessly navigate life? Jesus calls for an exchange of my personal style of relating for a biblical style of relating. It is an exchange of exposing my personal theology to a biblical theology. It is often painful and counterintuitive.

DRIVING IN SOUTH AFRICA

Learning to drive in South Africa was difficult for me. A different side of the car to drive from, a different side of the road to drive on. It was the same mode of transportation but a totally different experience. It took effort to remember when turning right to stay left. More than once I turned head-on into traffic because innately I would move back to the right side of the road. Over time, paying attention to the new way of driving, I began to relax and feel somewhat natural on the left side of the road. The old way of driving was always present so that driving was an ever-present intentional experience but less and less effort had to be put into it.

The educational or transformation cycle is always the same no matter what we are learning or transforming to:

- Unconscious incompetence to
- Conscious incompetence to
- Conscious competence to
- Unconscious competence

First we are found in a state of unconscious incompetence. We are ignorant and don't know that we are. *The initial movement in transformation is becoming aware of our ignorance, which takes us to the second stage in achieving conscious incompetence.* We are now aware of our incompetence. The only thing that has changed is simply becoming self-aware. This step is far harder than most think it is. Remember what Epictetus said, "It is impossible for a man to learn what he thinks he already knows."[2]

Researchers David Dunning and Justin Kruger quantified this thought in establishing the Dunning-Kruger Effect.[3] Basically, in experiments with college students, they demonstrated that our greatest enemy is not what we know but what we don't know that we don't know. To make matters worse, Dunning and Kruger demonstrated that the less competent we are the more likely we are to make this mistake. To put it another way, the less aware we are of our incompetence, the more likely we are to overestimate our competence. The untalented singers we love to cringe at in the audition rounds of *American Idol* aptly demonstrate that!

The third stage is the hard work of choosing to build habits based on our new awareness. Constant volitional action toward a new and different future leads to the fourth level. Unconscious competence is the natural state of living without much energy toward the new behavior. It becomes the normal natural way to think or action to take.

How does this relate to the spiritual journey? Our personal styles of relating are just that—personal, handcrafted. They serve us well because we craft them as our personal histories unfold. We become attached to them, much like a drowning victim becomes attached to a life-saving ring. Personal styles of relating feel like life-saving devices.

Expose these lifesaving devices to a biblical style of relating and trouble can arise. If conflict avoidance fits my personal style of relating because I grew up in a home where conflict was never constructive, I learn to avoid it at all cost. When I begin to follow Jesus, I learn that He said, "If one of your brothers or sisters sins against you: go to him, in private, and tell him just what you perceive the wrong to be" (Matt. 18:15). My personal style of relating and a biblical style of relating come to blows. Now who am I going to trust? Me, who has gotten myself this far, or Jesus, who is saying something so counter-intuitive to my personal style of relating that trusting Him seems to lead me toward self-destruction? This is the essence of the movement in the spiritual journey.

Just like learning to drive on a different side of the road, I must move through the internal turmoil required to allow the truth of the Bible to move me from unconsciously incompetent to consciously incompetent. I may not trust Jesus yet, but at least now I know that I do not. Nothing has changed in my emotions or actions, but I've made a giant leap forward overcoming the Dunning-Kruger Effect. I now know that I am incompetent.

That is the nature of the spiritual journey and why it is important to keep in mind how hard the journey can be. Many people start on a spiritual journey to find relief, peace of mind, or to overcome a sense of guilt or shame. When they discover that the journey consists of turmoil and even pain, it tests whether they are really seeking a connection to God or just wanting relief from their personal pain. Most of the people we work with have to come to the conclusion that they are lost before they can be found. It takes time to see the big picture of a righteous and just God and understand how personal choices have interrupted a family relationship with Him.

EXPLORING THE 7 JOURNEYS

When people visit a Shoal Creek service instead of attempting an assimilation program that connects them to the vision and values of Shoal Creek, we seek to connect them to God. The old pre-Reformation ministry style just builds dependence that makes replication difficult. The more moving parts you add to the disciple-making process the more complex it becomes. Complexity is not reproducible.

So we tell people that the spiritual journey consists of reading, obeying, and sharing the Bible. We offer them group opportunities and a path through the Bible—7 Journeys—that will take them through the seven major disciplines of the spiritual journey. They learn how to read, obey, and share the Bible in a Discovery Group (started by a friend, neighbor, or workmate) or a Journey Group (started by Shoal Creek on a semester schedule). In each of these groups, they have the chance to facilitate the discovery process and even host the group in their home or office (see chap. 6).

Both groups, Journey and Discovery, are encouraged to multiply and not to grow. Accomplishing the discovery process in ninety minutes is difficult with more than five people in the group, so adding group members becomes problematic. Starting new groups is the key. Willingness to multiply helps make clear whether or not group members are motivated to grow toward God. The discovery process, which is the operating system of the group, is designed to equip every member of the group to repeat the process. The vision of replication—finding people where they live, learn, work, and play who are spiritually interested and inviting them to join together to read the Bible and discover what God has to say about life—becomes reality when members of groups start their own groups.

Both groups, Journey and Discovery, are encouraged to multiply and not to grow.

The genius of what we've learned resides in the simplicity. NO other books or curriculum than the Bible. NO other subject-matter experts other than the Bible. Focusing on obedience is the goal of looking at the Bible. Igniting excitement about growing toward God stimulates sharing with others. Replication begins at that point.

The genius of discipling pre-believers is found in not having to change the process. There is no two-step evangelism where people are first encouraged to change their belief system and then their behavioral system. They simply begin to obey what God says and allow that truth to penetrate the key areas of their seven spiritual journeys. The seamless and simple moves from earner to heir, self-hearted to soft-hearted, receiver to giver, isolation to community, consumer to producer, charitable to extravagant, and traveler to guide sets a disciple up to be a disciple-maker—it makes disciple-making disciples!

The process of making disciple-making disciples is not a human activity, although humans are involved. It starts with a personal God who has made provisions for this relationship to develop. He made us in His image so we can communicate with Him. He encased some of His wisdom in a book we call the Bible. God the Spirit comes to us to empower our minds and bodies as we learn to walk with God.

This journey is one person growing to know and trust another. It requires constant exchange of meaning to allow the relationship to grow. Our Western minds want to compartmentalize that exchange of meaning into a box called *prayer*. It is unfortunate that we cordon off our communication with God into this box. In a Hebrew way of thinking, people relate to their Father in a moment-by-moment basis, not in a compartmentalized box. As we move in and out of the journeys, we hear from God and we ask, plead, cry out, share, complain, and thank; just a few of the emotive words that describe our exchange of meaning with God. We are never out of earshot of His ever-present care for us, yet we often feel far from Him. The nature of our deepening relationship with God is found in giving regular attention to Him and accepting his ever present attention to us.

The 7 Journeys gives some texture to God's work in our lives and substance to our communication with Him as we grow to trust, obey, share, relate, serve, give, and disciple. You have to leave the old normal behind to engage a genuine journey to God through Jesus.

The list of passages is designed to help assimilate the story of God's creation, man's rebellion, God's provision for the rebellion, and how we can join God's mission in this world and the world to come. As people read and respond in obedience to the wisdom of God in small, understandable, and livable sections, small steps of obedience walk them right into the family of God.

The list given here is designed for those who have grown up in the Western materialistic world where the spiritual journey is often confused with civil religion or even a folk style of Christianity. Borrowing a list from others is a start, but every culture needs a specially designed reading list. Each culture has its own obstacles in relating to the God of the Bible. For instance, because materialism is so prevalent in the suburbs of the United States, Shoal Creek's Bible reading list has the story of the rich, young ruler in it. Since money is the chief rival of God, becoming a disciple of Jesus needs to have that true in the path. The list of passages with each journey is just a beginning of a lifetime of pursuing God's wisdom. Each of these journeys has a plethora of Bible passages and concepts that can deepen and broaden our experience with God. Once you become accustomed to using a reading list, you are one step away from learning to develop a list on your own.

The rest of this chapter provides an in-depth look at the 7 Journeys process. Before reading further, review this short list of Bible passages to help prepare for the journey:

- Romans 12:1–2
- Psalm 8
- 2 Timothy 3:16–17
- Psalm 23
- 2 Peter 1:3–11
- Psalm 139:23–24
- Matthew 5:3–10

Every culture needs a specially designed reading list.

JOURNEY 1: EARNER TO HEIR—TRUST

Although we are created in God's image, possess dignity as a result, and are made to center our lives on Him, our rebellious hearts have separated us by seeking life apart from God. Our pursuit of a life apart from God includes any form of focus or energy that we use to organize our lives. This pursuit of life displays our depravity. It is not unusual to think of addiction or immorality in context with depravity. These certainly are a part of the picture, but family, serving, pursuit of comfort, and many other purposes or energies not often thought of as depravity make up a more holistic picture of substitute gods.

Adam and Eve, and subsequently all humanity, didn't just break the law. We are all, by nature, heart breakers. We've broken the heart of God by choosing to trust ourselves in the pursuit of life rather than trust Him. He designed Adam and Eve and their environment to provide the best life they could imagine. They wanted more and chose something else, breaking God's heart and the relationship they had with Him.

Because of His indescribable love for us, God freely yet painfully sent Jesus to restore our relationship despite His broken heart. Jesus' life, death, and resurrection paid the price for our reentry into God's family and made possible a life with God before death, not just after.

Because we've broken not just the law but God's heart—and you can't un-break a heart—we cannot do anything on our own to earn His favor. Instead, He graciously offers it to us so that we can be a part of His family. Our journey begins as we move from trusting our efforts and beginning to trust Jesus. No longer are we attempting to earn His favor, but we live as heirs of God's resources.

KEY BIBLE PASSAGE: TITUS 3:5–6

> [5]He came to save us. It's not that we earned it by doing good works or righteous deeds; He came because He is merciful. He brought us out of our old ways of living to a new beginning through the washing of regeneration; and He made us completely new through the

Holy Spirit, ⁶Who was poured out in abundance through Jesus the Anointed, our Savior.

MANTRA

You are worse off than you think but more loved
than you'll ever know.

BIBLE READING LIST:

- Genesis 1. There is a God, and He created the world and humans in His image.

- Genesis 3:1–19. The first humans disobey God and separate themselves from Him.

- Genesis 6:9–22. God grieves over human disobedience but provides a way of hope.

- Exodus 20:1–21. God gives His commandments to His people.

- Leviticus 4:1–7. God requires offerings for the disobedience of His people.

- Isaiah 53. God tells of the future suffering of the promised Savior.

- Hosea 3. Despite constant unfaithfulness, God provides a way back.

- Luke 2:1–20. Jesus is born according to predictions in the first half of Bible (Old Testament).

- Luke 5:17–26. Jesus has the authority to forgive our disobedience and to heal.

- John 3:1–18. Jesus is God's only Son, sent to bring us back to a life with God.

- Luke 15:11–32. God longs for our return to His family.

- Luke 18:18–25. Jesus wants us to understand the value of trusting Him.

- John 11:38–44. Jesus has authority over death.

- Luke 24: 36–49. Jesus died and came back to life to secure our forgiveness.

- Romans 5:1–11. Jesus' death and resurrection paid our debt to God and makes our return to God's family possible.

- Acts 1:1–11. Jesus will come back in the same way that He left.

- Acts 2:29–38. Believers respond by proclaiming their personal relationship publicly through repentance and baptism.

JOURNEY 2: SELF-HEARTED TO SOFT-HEARTED—OBEY

God desires a face-to-face relationship with each of us, one that grows from being me-centered to being God-centered as we read the Bible and obey what He says. Exploring the self-hearted inclinations of our souls and acknowledging and confessing our selfish desires opens the door for us to experience His forgiveness and live a soft-hearted life where what He says matters most.

The system of operation or personal style of relating needs to be washed regularly by the renewing of biblical truth. This habit further defines our allegiance to Jesus and because we obey His commands, it demonstrates that we aren't just "saved" but that we decided to follow him by obeying Him. As those commands become a part of our weekly experience, our personal styles of relating are confronted and transformed by the renewing power of God the Spirit.

Jesus defines for His disciples what it means to follow Him. Obedience to His commands shows the love and trust of one who recognizes Jesus as God who came to lead us back to our Father.

God desires a face-to-face relationship with each of us.

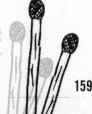

159

The spiritual journey is a lifelong process of identifying areas of hard-heartedness and allowing divine intervention to create a soft-hearted, obedient posture toward our Father in heaven.

KEY BIBLE PASSAGE: ROMANS 12:1–2

Brothers and sisters, in light of *all I have shared with you about* God's mercies, I urge you to offer your bodies as a living and holy sacrifice *to God*, a sacred offering that brings Him pleasure; this is your reasonable, essential worship. ²Do not allow this world to mold you in its own image. Instead, be transformed *from the inside out* by renewing your mind. As a result, you will be able to discern what God wills and whatever God finds good, pleasing, and complete.

MANTRA

What God says ought to matter most.

BIBLE READING LIST:

- Mark 7:17–23. God's work starts at our core and moves outward.
- Luke 9:23–25. Following Jesus is a life of surrender.
- Luke 18:9–14. True understanding of ourselves creates humility before God.
- Ephesians 2:1–10. We must recognize and attack our old way of thinking.
- 1 John 2:1–6. Obedience is God's love language.
- Psalm 119:24–33. What God says matters most.
- Romans 12:1–2. Surrender is doing God's will.
- Proverbs 3:5–6. Obedience is trusting God rather than self.
- 1 Corinthians 6:12–20. My body is God's dwelling place on this earth.

JOURNEY 3: RECEIVER TO GIVER—SHARE

Having been touched deeply by God's actions for us, it's only natural to share this good news with others. Benefiting from what we don't deserve births an infectious spirit of generosity. Since we didn't earn it, everyone has a chance to enjoy this newfound favor of the Creator. His mission to reach humanity with the transforming story of Jesus becomes our mission. The natural overflow of a life lived in obedience to God identifies publicly what is happening internally.

We begin to live our lives "out loud," expressing to those in our relational circles the change that God is making in our lives. God's love begins to transform our relationships. Just like one beggar showing another beggar where to find food, we share with our friends, neighbors, family, and coworkers how our lives are being changed.

Instead of sharing our faith with our friends, we learn to share our lives. Rather than pressure them to believe, we invite them to see our journey, both good and bad, up close and personal. This provides the platform to invite them to read the Bible and discover what God has to say about life.

KEY BIBLE PASSAGE: 2 CORINTHIANS 5:11–21

> [11]So because we stand in awe of the *one true* Lord, we make it our aim to convince all people *of the truth of the gospel*; God sees who we really are, and I hope *in some way* that you'll look deeply into your consciences to see us as well. [12]*But we hope you understand that* we are not trying to prove ourselves to you *or pull together a résumé that will impress you*. We are simply hoping that you will find a sense of joy in connecting with us. And when you are approached by others (who may value appearances more than the heart) *asking questions about us,* you will be able to offer an answer for them. [13]If we *seem out of control or* act like fanatics, it is for God. But if we act in a coherent and reasonable way, it is for you. [14]You see, the controlling force in our lives is the love of the Anointed One. And our confession is this: One died for all; therefore, all have died. [15]He died for us so that we will all live, not for ourselves, but

for Him who died and rose from the dead. [16]*Because of all that God has done,* we now have a new perspective. We used to show regard for people based on worldly standards and interests. No longer. We used to think of the Anointed the same way. No longer. [17]Therefore, if anyone is united with the Anointed One, that person is a new creation. The old life is gone—and see—a new life has begun! [18]All of this is *a gift* from *our Creator* God, who has *pursued us and* brought us into a restored *and healthy* relationship with Him through the Anointed. And He has given us *the same mission,* the ministry of reconciliation, *to bring others back to Him.* [19]*It is central to our good news that* God was in the Anointed making things right between Himself and the world. This means He does not hold their sins against them. But it also means He charges us to proclaim the message that heals and restores our broken relationships *with God and each other.*

[20]So we are now representatives of the Anointed One, *the Liberating King;* God has given us a charge to carry through our lives— urging all people on behalf of the Anointed to become reconciled to *the Creator* God. [21]He orchestrated this: the *Anointed* One, who had never experienced sin, became sin for us so that in Him we might embody the very righteousness of God.

MANTRA

Lost people matter to God, so they ought to
matter to me.

BIBLE READING LIST:

- Matthew 28:16–20. Go teach the world to obey Jesus.
- 2 Corinthians 5:16–21. We are to join God in reconciling the world.
- Matthew 5:13–16. Serving others brings to light the change in us.
- 1 Corinthians 9:19–23. The mission should mold our relationships.

- Luke 10:1–11. Jesus calls us to the spiritually interested.
- Acts 1:6–8. All of Jesus' followers are ordained to share His message.
- John 4:27–35. People are ready to hear about reconnecting with the Father in heaven.
- Luke 19:1–10. Jesus came to find and reconnect people to God
- Matthew 9:35–38. Jesus viewed people as helpless and harassed.

JOURNEY 4: ISOLATION TO COMMUNITY—RELATE

Being created in the image of a triune God (Father, Son, and Holy Spirit), we are made for a life in community with other image bearers. Even with all our connectedness these days, isolation is pervasive. The truth is we grow more, we laugh and cry more, we love more when we are relating deeply with others. Life was made to be lived together.

People don't need to know the details of my life, but I have a need for them to! James 5:16 encourages us to talk about our failings with our friends. The favor afforded us by God gives us the freedom to explore our personal styles of relating and share our depravity with our spiritual family. Galatians 6 shows us how to create communities of grace that provide a vision for God's heart in our lives and the ability to address when we fall short. As the isolation of the soul is broken, strength from community grows.

Loneliness and isolation are enemies of the life God intended because we have a spiritually designed need to connect with others. Truly getting to know others and engaging with them is vital. Life change happens best in authentic accountable relationships.

KEY BIBLE PASSAGE: HEBREWS 10:24–25

> [24]Let us consider how to inspire each other to greater love and to righteous deeds, [25]not forgetting to gather as a community, as some

have forgotten, but encouraging each other, especially as the day of
His return approaches.

MANTRA

*Made in the image of God, I was designed to live
in community.*

BIBLE READING LIST:

- Mark 2:1–12. Sacrifice and commitment mark relationships of Jesus' followers.

- Hebrews 10:24–25. Building relationships that agitate is essential to the spiritual journey.

- Philippians 2:3–8. Jesus' sacrifice sets the standard for our relating.

- Ecclesiastes 4:9–10. Strength is found in relationships, not in isolation.

- Acts 2:41–47. Life together focused on the Bible sustains a life of healthy community.

- John 13:34–35. When love defines our relationship, Jesus is recognized as our leader

- 1 Peter 1:13–23. The quality of our relationships with one another defines us as Jesus' followers.

- Ephesians 4:20–29. As children of God we reflect His manner of relating in the way we relate.

- Romans 12:9–21. Obedience to Jesus is seen in our relating to others with love.

JOURNEY 5: CONSUMER TO PRODUCER– SERVE

The Bible says Jesus came to serve not to be served. He didn't enter
the world entitled to all the rights and privileges accorded God.

Philippians 2 describes His attitude of humility, willing to put aside even His claim to be God in an effort to serve. Paul urged us (2:5) to have the same serving attitude as Jesus. As God's children, made in His image and on a mission to expand His kingdom, we, too, are made to serve. Jesus gave us a key to life when He suggested the counterintuitive principle of finding our lives by losing them (Luke 17:33). Life is not found in the collection of comfort, conveniences, or cash but by finding our places to serve in God's mission on this earth.

God has given all followers unique and special resources. One of our lifelong goals should be to discover and employ those resources by serving to bring heaven to earth. The act of giving away our time and talents to benefit others becomes a discipline that nurtures our spiritual lives. Finding a place to serve others is critical—not to them, but to us.

KEY BIBLE PASSAGE: 1 PETER 4:7–11

[7]We are coming to the end of all things, so be serious and keep your wits about you in order to pray *more forcefully*. [8]Most of all, love each other steadily and unselfishly, because love makes up for many faults. [9]Show hospitality to each other without complaint. [10]Use whatever gift you've received *for the good of* one another so that you can show yourselves to be good stewards of God's grace in all its varieties. [11]If you're called upon to talk, speak as though God put the words in your mouth; if you're called upon to serve others, serve as though you had the strength of God behind you. In these ways, God may be glorified in all you do through Jesus the Anointed, to whom belongs glory and power, now and forever. Amen.

God has given all followers unique and special resources.

MANTRA

Life is found in giving it away.

BIBLE READING LIST:

- ☙ Luke 12:13–21. The abundant life Jesus promised is a life that is rich toward God.

- ☙ Luke 8:4–15. The fruitfulness of my life is determined by the nature of my obedience.

- ☙ Romans 12:3–8. I must use the gifts God has given me to experience the riches of His family.

- ☙ Luke 19:10–27. I am entrusted by God as His steward of this world and my gifts.

- ☙ 1 Peter 4:7–11. God's gifts are to be used for His purposes for His kingdom.

- ☙ Galatians 3:26–29. There is no caste system in God's family. All are heirs.

- ☙ 1 Peter 2:1–9. God calls His family to be priests and spread His message.

- ☙ Matthew 28:16–20. We are all called to the process of making disciple-making disciples.

- ☙ 1 Corinthians 12:1–12. We are called to invest what God has given us for His purposes.

JOURNEY 6: CHARITABLE TO EXTRAVAGANT—GIVE

At our core is a battle for control. Jesus said we have to choose between God and money, something especially difficult for those in developed countries where money is the chief rival god. Its presence creates trust issue for humans. The presence of wealth attracts comfort. Its absence exposes those trust issues as anxiety rises.

God's extravagant love for us empowers us to be extravagant in our giving. Giving is an act of trust in the giver of every good and perfect gift (James 1:17). He trusts us with His stuff, and we in turn demonstrate our love and trust of Him by generously redistributing His gifts for his mission. He lends us His resources while on this earth and gives us the opportunity to express our trust in Him by giving generously to the expansion of Jesus' cause. What a privilege to partner with God by investing in His work in our world! Our spiritual journey is vitally connected to the way we handle the resources God entrusts to us.

KEY BIBLE PASSAGE: 2 CORINTHIANS 9:6–8

> ⁶But I will say this to encourage your generosity: the one who plants little harvests little, and the one who plants plenty harvests plenty. ⁷Giving grows out of the heart—otherwise, you've reluctantly grumbled "yes" because you felt you had to or because you couldn't say "no," *but this isn't* the way God wants it. *For we know that* "God loves a cheerful giver." ⁸God is ready to overwhelm you with more blessings than you could ever imagine so that you'll always be taken care of in every way and you'll have more than enough to share.

MANTRA

If there is anything I have I can't give away, I don't own it; it owns me.

BIBLE READING LIST:

- ❧ Romans 8:31–32. God demonstrates a generous heart in the gift of His Son.
- ❧ Matthew 6:19–24. We can trust God with everything we have because He shows Himself trustworthy.

- Luke 18:18–25. Money is a rival of God that can keep us from God's family.

- 2 Corinthians 9:6–15. Our generosity is a natural reflection of what God is doing to and for us.

- Ecclesiastes 2:1–11. Life's pursuit apart from God leads to futility.

- Proverbs 6:6–11. Preparation and frugality are the signs of God's control of our money.

- 1 Timothy 6:6–10. The desire for money can rob us from a life with God.

- Mark 12:41–44. Great sacrifice comes out of our poverty.

- 2 Corinthians 8:1–7. It is a privilege and responsibility to give to God's work.

JOURNEY 7: TRAVELER TO GUIDE—DISCIPLE

God plans to spread His message to the ends of the earth through His followers—not a special class of followers, not specially trained followers, but every ordinary follower. He ordains the ordinary! As His disciples, we have the privilege and responsibility to influence the growth of others, not as experts or clergy, but as guides, always pointing the way to Jesus.

While physical infertility can be a painful journey for a married couple who wishes to have children, infertility in the spiritual realm is unthinkable in Jesus' mind. Every follower of Jesus experiences a rebirth for the express purpose of reproducing. We were born to reproduce! This is the natural outcome of learning to love God and obey Jesus. There is no greater love of God and others than to replicate the life of God in others.

God plans to spread His message to the ends of the earth through His followers.

The further you move on this journey, the more you realize your role in God's work is not about you, but about others. We are responsible to pass along to others the experience, skills, and opportunities that have been entrusted to us. God intends for us to join Him in making disciple-making disciples so the good news can reach the ends of the earth.

KEY BIBLE PASSAGE: MATTHEW 28:19–20

> [19]Go out and make disciples in all the nations. Ceremonially wash them through baptism in the name of the *triune* God: Father, Son, and Holy Spirit. [20]Then disciple them. Form them in the practices and postures that I have taught you, and show them how to follow the commands I have laid down for you. And I will be with you, day after day, to the end of the age.

MANTRA

I was made to reproduce.

BIBLE READING LIST:

- Matthew 28:16–20. Disciple-making is normal for the follower of Christ.

- Luke14:25–33. Access to life with God requires a death on a daily basis.

- 2 Timothy 2:1–7. Following Jesus means impacting the lives of others.

- John 15:1–8. Essential to making disciple-makers is learning to stay connected to the source of fruit bearing.

- Matthew 5:3–12. Transforming the internal character of a disciple is crucial to the making of disciple-makers.

- 2 Corinthians 5:16–20. We have the privilege of joining God as He reconciles the world to Himself.

- Hebrews 5:11–14. Full devotion and regular growth are normal for the follower of Christ.
- Matthew 7:21–27. Doing what Jesus said is the litmus test of a disciple-making disciple.

This life therefore is not righteousness, but growth in righteousness, not health, but healing, not being but becoming, not rest but exercise. We are not yet what we shall be, but we are growing toward it, the process is not yet finished, but it is going on, this is not the end, but it is the road. All does not yet gleam in glory, but all is being purified.[4]

Martin Luther

LEADERSHIP LESSONS FROM AN UNLIKELY PLACE

FROM MARKETER TO REVOLUTIONARY

I hope this book has piqued your interest in exploring the idea of multiplicative disciple-making. If so, I suggest that you read and reread this chapter.

One of the gravest mistakes you can make is to implement a new strategy in old ways. Jesus phrased this as putting new wine into old wine skins (Mark 2:22). It has the same success rate as finding a cool new app for an iPhone and trying to get it on an Android—two different platforms built on two different languages. Even though they share some things in common, they are not compatible, nor will things designed for one work on the other.

We've learned to push new ideas through organizations with a marketer's mentality. We can harness our communication channels, key personnel, and creative drive for new programs that take us in new directions. We turn up the volume in our main communication channels, reduce the clutter of other information to create clarity, and persist with a constant message. This works—we see examples in our everyday life. It even works in the church with semester-based group structures, campaign strategies, and recruitment of volunteers.

What this book offers, however, is not a new program that can be implemented. It is establishing a new culture, a new way of thinking about an old idea—a disciple-making culture. Culture building takes time. Language needs to be developed, mind shifts need to be experienced, and skills need to be learned. Adherents can't just know the names of the new labels; they need to understand the whys of the words they are learning.

> It is establishing a new culture, a new way of thinking about an old idea.

You can use a marketer's tactics to implement a multiplicative disciple-making strategy in an existing organization, but it will have a life cycle like any other program. When it is new, there will be energy and excitement, but as the newness wears off so will the excitement. Eventually it will be replaced by something newer and more exciting. That's what happens with things that are marketed.

We are not offering a new program. We are contemplating a new way of thinking and acting with the good news toward a world on its way to a Christ-less eternity. Building a culture takes time, especially since this isn't a new construction project but a re-construction project. There are old ways of thinking to tear down and new ways to be explored.

If the old adage in remodeling—it takes twice as long and costs twice as much—applies here, and I think it does, this will require patience, perseverance, and a new metaphor.

Let's start with the metaphor. Instead of the classic marketing mentality, we should look at terrorist movements. This may seem wrong at first, but think for a moment about who has had the most impact on your life in the past fifteen years. If you travel at all, it's terrorists. There was a day when you could arrive at an airport thirty minutes to an hour early and be there in plenty of time. That day no longer exists. The terrorists from 9/11 have caused us to need to get to an airport up to two hours in advance to stand in a long line and take our shoes off, get our laptops out, remove our jackets, and stand with our hands over our heads to be scanned.

Turn on the news and you can't go thirty minutes without some terrorist organization around the world being mentioned. Conflicts in the Middle East, south Asia, and Africa are fueled by these amorphous organizations that elude traditional policing practices. For lack of a better word, terrorists have the most effective organizations existing today, as it pertains to how they have affected everyone around them.

Jesus used the power of divine love, the model of His life and His unity with the Father to motivate change in our lives.

Jesus was a revolutionary. His strategy was so ingenious that it not only survived but thrived through the first three centuries after His death. Reengaging His way of thinking gives us the best chance to change a culture.

Thinking counterintuitively like a revolutionary, not unlike Jesus, has at least four separate elements:

1. You need to be radically committed to cause.

2. You need to start at the fringes, not at the front.

3. You need to start small.

4. You must persevere by learning to fail faster and smarter.

As a church planter, I was always hungry for new ideas that will grow the church. Seven years ago when our target changed from 300 thousand to 2.5 million, our thinking about church, church growth, and how we measured success changed. We no longer could be satisfied with the idea of growing a church; we became committed to growing "The Church." Just because we were succeeding at reaching the lost didn't give us the right to be smug about all those who weren't. We, The Church, are a team and if we don't succeed, no one succeeds.

Here is the litmus test: If I can equip you with a new way of thinking and acting about the Great Commission, and if this will not add one volunteer to your church, dollar to your offering plate, or attender to your church services, but does grow Jesus' kingdom, would you be interested? Don't kid yourself here because the answer to this question is vital to your success in implementing any kind of multiplicative disciple-making strategy.

Pastors and church staffs are not paid to cause the kingdom to grow away from them. They are paid to grow it toward them so it can be measured, celebrated, and remunerated. So a positive answer to this question puts you in a countercultural, often counter local church stance. In some environments, a positive answer might even lead to unemployment.

Radical change requires radical commitment. Before you begin to bring others on the journey, make sure you understand this journey thoroughly and are developing your bone-deep commitment to this cause. It is not enough to be curious or frustrated with the status quo. At some point having a Popeye moment—"I can't stands it anymore!"—leads to the passionate and thoughtful pursuit of a new way of thinking or acting about the Great Commission.

CHANGING THE WINE SKINS

In my case, it took three years! I tracked down David Watson, coauthor of Contagious Disciple-Making and anyone else talking about multiplicative disciple-making. I found David Broodryk, a Watson disciple, while I was in Africa, to give a workshop to some folks I was working with. I reread the Gospels and book of Acts. I studied Paul's journeys to see if what they were saying could possibly be true. I traveled to meetings where I could talk with these guys face-to-face and challenge them with my questions. Like an onion, my layers slowly began to peel back and my vision cleared as I began learning to read the Bible without my cultural bias. I've already delineated the mental shifts in a previous chapter, but let's do a quick review:

- From evangelizing to conversion to discipling to conversion
- From knowledge-focused to obedience-focused disciple-making
- From making disciples to making disciple-making disciples
- From trusting the qualified to releasing the willing
- From reproduction to replication
- From less concerned about what I am saying to more concerned about what they are thinking
- From telling people what to think to suggesting what they should be thinking about
- From measuring inputs to measuring outcomes
- From being a communicator to being a learning designer
- From being concerned about becoming more radical to being irrationally committed to being simple

Some of these shifts were welcomed like the sun on a frosty winter's day, while others came through long nights of labor pains. To suggest that I have "arrived" would be a gross misuse of the word. I have really only begun to make this move. I've learned to live in a discomforting world where all of my natural theological tendencies are under scrutiny. It is a learning posture that I am growing to enjoy despite the discomfort.

I am committed, irrationally so. If it takes working at Starbucks to earn a living, I want to catalyze movements of multiplicative disciple-making before I die. I want to help transition this disciple-making movement thinking from rural to urban. You must spend the time it takes to explore, discover, and commit to the development of a new culture of multiplicative disciple-making. This journey is not for the faint of heart!

Discovering the revolutionary thinking gives us a clue where to start once we are on the journey of commitment. They don't shout from the front room, they work on the fringes. Their work is unseen for the longest time. They are not interested in being popular or spending time developing logos, brochures, or tag lines.

They look for the disenfranchised, those who exist on the edges, for people without a voice. Every church or Christian organization has a group of "holy discontents." I am

They get excited about moving beyond the traditional structures of the church.

not talking about the complainers and those who can't seem to be satisfied by any move that a local church makes. Holy discontent is usually measured by those who have a vision of what could happen but feel that the existing structures prevent them from acting or don't give them permission to act. They generally are people who are actively serving outside the existing structures yet feel that this service is not acknowledged or is even frowned upon by their church leaders. As a result of their external focus, the holy discontented usually have more relationships with the unbelieving world than does the average church attender.

The disenfranchised crowd provides the team that a revolutionary looks for. They are ripe for a new way of thinking and doing. Small, private conversations about what could be lights a fire in their eyes. They are the makings of a new culture, the new wineskins just waiting for the new wine. They don't have to be motivated to move; they get excited about moving beyond the traditional structures of the church.

Call them to small, private practices of this new culture as the next step in building a disciple-making culture. Churches tend to talk about new things rather than do new things. Teaching people to use the discovery process in their own lives and to begin to press the good news into their relational networks outside the existing church creates the first of many exciting movements. It is these kind of folks who gravitate to a discipled life.

DON'T GROW; MULTIPLY

There is no harm in using the discovery process with friendly faces. But getting outside of your current Christian context will bring energy that is hard for you to imagine. So meet and use the discovery process, but pray and strategize about calling your friends who aren't enjoying the family of God at the moment. Ask them to join you at the table to read the Bible together to learn what God has to say about life.

After a few weeks of meeting and reading the Bible as an internal catalyst group, establish the principle that all sharing will be done with those whose spiritual journeys you are unsure about. This focus on the lost will either make or break your group. If, after three or four weeks, group members fail to find people who are lost, you are probably working with the wrong people. Don't be discouraged—it is not unusual for a Christian to have no non-Christian friends. It also takes lots of tries to get this into practice. Just like learning anything else, there is a period of failure that precedes success.

Here is a mistake that most people make when first engaging disciple-making movement strategies: they see the discovery process and how it gets people's fingerprints on the Bible, and they think that's the secret sauce. Simply opening up the Bible isn't the secret sauce. Not that it isn't significant, but by itself it will not ignite movements of disciple-making disciples unless, of course, God decides to do so. To build a culture that fosters multiplicative disciple-making, you have to think differently.

We are talking about building a culture: a system of operation built on principles left by Jesus for us to follow. Allowing God to be the teacher and using discovery as the key element of transformation is but one of several key cultural pillars that movements are built on.

In practical terms, this means that you can meet with your catalyst group to do the discovery process around the Bible, but you also need to time to reprogram their thinking.

The whys of thinking differently take time and repeated discussion to get through to people. "Why don't I start a group in my home? I have the gift of hospitality." Because my friend, your gift of hospitality may keep someone from heaven! Not everyone has the gift of hospitality, so the treats that you serve, the cleanliness of your house, the value of your house, or even the location of your house can be an obstacle for someone starting a group that could reach friends, relatives, or workmates.

The whys underneath groups multiplying instead of growing will need to be rehearsed over and over. Concepts such as *relationship* and *community* will become enemies to movements. Early in our practice, even though we trained our group facilitators to keep the groups small and multiply rather than grow, we failed. A very successful group facilitator, who had genuine nonbelieving neighbors reading the Bible, allowed the group to grow, fearing that by multiplying they might cause a neighbor to feel left out. The group doubled in size and began running into problems actually getting to the Bible reading and obedience statements. Slowly it dissolved into a group getting together to expose their lives to one another.

There is nothing wrong with that except that the facilitator had hoped to see neighbors find trust in a heavenly Father rather than a safe place to complain about their spouses. Since there are so few places to find that safe place, community can become a lethal injection to the spread of the good news. A group interested in multiplicative disciple-making needs to have frequent and repeated discussions about these issues to get to generational growth (groups multiplying into new groups).

PAY ATTENTION TO THE ROOTS

Starting at the fringes rather than the front sets you up for the best possible long-term success. Involve your coconspirators in practicing the discovery process and rehearsing the principle of movement-thinking. The tendency is to want to involve the entire Sunday School, Adult Bible fellowship, or Small Group ministry in the discovery process: the front of the room. The front of the room is very appealing because of the illusion of power. We think we can turn the ship on a dime. But every church, whether it has five hundred people or has been in existence for fifty years, is more like an aircraft carrier than a catamaran. It just doesn't quickly turn effectively. Trying to do so with a radical departure from established methods invites trouble.

The front of the room in a typical church or organization seduces us into thinking that we can roll out this latest, greatest ministry strategy in a big way. Even if we have attrition, we'll still have critical mass to keep this rolling. Fight against this with every fiber of your being. That doesn't mean you can't announce publically that a group is exploring some new ways of discipling. But don't bet your paycheck that public announcements and marketing will get you where you want to go. It is better to start small. Consider a test group. This will allow you to fail in obscurity. There is nothing within Christianity that prompts a more allergic reaction than failure. You need a place and time to experiment. Regardless of your feelings of competency, I can tell you from experience that you won't know what you are doing. You will need a coach and a mentor. A coach will help you with the skills you need to develop, and a mentor will help you process the internal turmoil that will develop.

Regular inquiries by church leaders into Shoal Creek's strategy come with this question: How's it working for you? Ultimately, that

You need a place and time to experiment.

question is parsed into numbers. My answers are usually unsatisfactory to the inquirer. They want to hear eye-popping numbers that in turn will pique their interest to explore a multiplicative disciple-making strategy. Success comes from starting small, at the fringes, and following God's leading.

I refuse to give out numbers because of a personal conviction. We didn't head down this road because we went to a conference and heard that so-and-so had this many groups. We became convinced that the principles we discovered working in other cultures were biblical. Success was and isn't our scorecard. We are convinced that this is the way that Jesus taught.

Every Disciple-Making Movement I know of has an underground story, a time when roots are grown. Before you hear of the tens of thousands being baptized and the thousands of churches that are planted, there are starts and restarts. However, each of these starts and restarts is replete with serious failures that never seem to get chronicled. Stories that tell of the success rarely have room for the mistakes, such as working with the wrong people, failing to understand the cancer of dependency, inadequate coaching care, hidden agendas that arise at inopportune times . . . the list goes on.

What I've learned is that, as my mind-set shifts started, the skills were more art than science. Learning to recruit, equip, and coach was more organic that mechanistic. It wasn't until I had tried and failed or even partially succeeded that I learned. Watching my first unregenerate person facilitate a Discovery Group challenged my theological paradigms and was emotionally exhausting. Once I experienced it, my mind shifts made sense. The process is so simple and repeatable; as long as the Bible is the authority even a pre-Christian can facilitate.

You can talk about that issue, argue it from your theological framework, but once you experience it you can actually feel what Paul wrote about in Romans 1:16: "It is God's power to save every person who believes."

Keep it small, and you'll have the opportunity to risk big and fail small. You won't load your detractors' guns for them. When I say small, I mean somewhere between six and twenty people split up into groups of no more than five who are regularly practicing the discovery process and meeting to pray, learn, and strategize about seeing the gospel move.

At Shoal Creek, we developed a course that culminates in the formation of a Disciple-Making Movement Learning Community (DMLC). Over a nine-week period, a group can wander through the key areas and learn the basics while having a chance to practice. Just as in the discovery process, the more people get involved the more likely they are to be changed by the process.

> If you stay small and personal, you don't need formal approval by a board.

Generally, if you stay small and personal, you don't need formal approval by a board. The biggest mistake that many people make is to take the idea of multiplicative disciple-making to a board with the naive confidence that the governance structures will get behind this. This is not the wisest move for two reasons. First, those taking this issue to a board aren't the most informed about what they are proposing. Second, there are many counterintuitive issues in multiplicative disciple-making that can't be addressed as an item on a board agenda.

Stay under the radar and away from any need to get formal approval. It allows you to have stories to go along with a theory when and if you do decide to make a formal presentation. There is nothing to be gained by having a governing board take action. Don't let your excitement for getting closer to the Great Commission lead you to pursue unwise directions. Get a few people and get started.

Since we share the same truth but different contexts, everything has to be tailored. Having a small group to work through the tailoring process is extremely helpful. You need to tailor the discovery questions. For instance, take the fourth question, "Do you have a need or does someone you know have a need that this group could meet?" While working with folks in South Africa, we discovered that the word *need* raised a lot of issues because, in a poverty-driven culture, everyone is in need. So the wording of the question needed to focus on the community and not the individual, to help them get their eyes on the needs in the community.

You'll need to think about a list of Bible passages that will lead someone to take a position in God's family. What issues in your culture need to be addressed so that people can pledge their allegiance to God and God alone? Jesus didn't think this was a post-conversion topic, so we follow His lead and have our pre-Christians read and obey this passage on their way to God's family.

The fewer moving parts you have at the beginning, the better. Don't let the American addiction to finding success in numbers pervert your thinking. Remember, you don't want to put new wine into old wineskins.

MAKE FRIENDS WITH FAILURE

Last, but certainly not least, is your partnership with failure. Because this is more art than science, your major learning will not come from the manual, but from experience. You have to change your relationship with failure. It is not your enemy; it is your mentor. Moving away from failure as if it is contagious robs us of the amazing mentor it can become. If we have an allergic reaction to failure, it is as if we pay the tuition for the course but don't get credit for it. That wouldn't be smart!

Every attempt at anything—from starting a group, multiplying a group, making spiritual statements to friends, or attempting to coach someone—needs a postmortem. Ask some basic questions of every experience to make sure that failure is accompanied by learning. Adopt an attitude of failing faster and smarter. It creates a posture of learning that will make us dangerous for Jesus' kingdom. We simply ask:

- What did we do right?
- What did we do wrong?
- What would we do differently?

This provides a simple, doable postmortem that doesn't become overly critical yet allows us to get to the learning moment from the experience.

A last responsibility in regards to learning from failure is learning to capture and communicate the lessons. The adage, "The group is smarter than the individual" is true only when we create an environment of sharing knowledge. I long for the day when we have a Wikipedia for Disciple-Making Movements. Until then, make sure your team members share their knowledge quickly and freely. Capture that learning someplace so that as people join you they can learn from past failures.

The adventure we are on at Shoal Creek has more people reading, obeying, and sharing what God is up to in their lives than at any time in our history. It is exciting to see people gain confidence in hearing from God for themselves. Amazing God-sized things can happen. We are still underground in our story. We are more convinced than ever of our direction. We hope we can get more people walking alongside us to learn with us. We've always loved the bleeding edge, but we'd love some company out here. See appendix C, "What the Future Could Look Like."

WHAT KIND OF CHURCH?

One of the most frequent questions I get asked is, "Where do you see this going in the future?" At Shoal Creek, our hope is that our hybrid strategy will allow us to be a "server" church. This idea comes from the technical world. Every organization that has a digital footprint has a server. It is a system of software and hardware components that allocates resources for devices to access the internet, store, retrieve, or communicate data.

We use laptops, iPhones, Androids, iPads, surfaces, tablets, even desktops to access a server. It doesn't matter the size, make, or type of device, the server is able to provide resources for them all. In that relationship, the server is able to allocate the appropriate resources for the appropriate device. Seamlessly, the server works behind the scenes to allow the network to be stable, grow, and exchange the information needed to serve the network's purposes.

> **There are plenty of people who still need some type of a formal structure to pursue their spiritual journeys.**

Our hope is to be a server church that can resource any number of expressions of biblically functioning community. We are convinced that we don't have to be jealous for these investments to return to us in any way, in people attending or in dollars to support the cause.

There are plenty of people who still need some type of a formal structure to pursue their spiritual journeys. But there are also just as many who will never use a formal religious structure to pursue God. We have a responsibility to both.

I welcome the uncertain future with hope that it is a mind-bending collage of house churches, neighborhood churches, churches planted at work, on campuses, in gyms, on traveling sports teams, online—anywhere someone who needs to connect to God can be found. My hope is:

- the forms will follow function so that we are more focused on making disciple-making disciples than we are arguing about incarnational strategies, missional communities, reformed theology, or ecclesiology.

- that these churches made up of disciple-making disciples will have the freedom to develop forms that support and encourage their functions.

- for the building of obedience-focused, self-replicating, disciple-making communities that continue to move through where we live, learn, work, and play, seeing the Great Commission fulfilled in my lifetime.

MOVEMENT-READY PEOPLE

JUMP!

What will it take to see Disciple-Making Movements in the West? I've heard that question hundreds of times and asked it many times myself. To accurately understand the answer, we need to confront the nature of movements and catalysts who respond to God's leading when He ignites them.

When I first began my journey into multiplicative disciple-making, the term *CPM*, or Church Planting Movements, was described in various terms of specificity but generally was viewed as a rapid replication of indigenous churches planting churches within a given people group or population segment that moves to four generations in a short period of time.

Several issues challenged me very quickly. The definition was clearly biased to a frontier missional situation. The real red flag popped up when I saw that all of the players, experiences, and practices were developed in rural settings in emerging countries. Cultural questions were first on the table.

Family-oriented, poverty-laden contexts birthed these movements. My context was materialistically laden, with a messed up family structure. Were these methods successful because of cultural elements? Was it possible to translate these methods to the West? Would economic, educational, and religious factors negate the impact of these methods in my context?

The second lump in my throat came with the use of the word *church*. What I was hearing described sounded more like small groups than a church. I had a hard time reconciling the terminology. Using my patterns of thinking, I wondered if they were talking about starting house churches or some type of small-group network.

Most of these questions were resolved by moving back into the Bible and reading it without my Western eyes. But the CPM-Church Planting Movements resolved itself. Early in my engagement, there was a change to Disciple-Making Movements (DMM). Because the word *church* is laden with Western cultural trappings, people couldn't conceive of forty thousand churches being planted in the space of fourteen years. Their concept of church was significantly different from those that were planted in Bhojpuri—not biblically different but culturally different.

Even though the adaptation to DMM is not universal, it seems that for those of us in the West who are working in a culture with a fixed and polluted understanding of *church*, we are better served by the term DMM rather than CPM. It alleviates the unnecessary discussions erupting at the beginning and focuses us on the Great Commission.

COUNTERINTUITIVE MOVES

The transition to a new way of thinking took some *counterintuitive* moves in my mentality. I've used that term many times in this book as well as giving several examples. It's so important that we understand the nature of the decisions we have to make. Using our current patterns of thinking we often make decisions that just don't look intelligent. They look downright self-annihilating.

Wagner Dodge faced the cost of introducing counterintuitive thinking with his fire crew during the Mann Gulch fire in 1949. His crew of fifteen smoke jumpers was tasked with fighting a fire on a 97-degree day in high winds. The fire was so hot that they couldn't get within one hundred feet of it. While trying to figure out where to start fighting the fire, it turned on them and quickly they were in emergency evacuation mode.

After several attempts to find an escape path, Wagner decided on a counterintuitive strategy. He commanded his men to abandon their heavy gear. He started a circular fire. The fire burned bare a small patch of ground about one hundred feet in diameter. He ordered his men into the middle of the circle. In the fired frenzy of a life-and-death situation most of his men ignored the order and chose to find their own escape routes: thirteen of them died trying to find their way out. Wagner Dodge survived.

His counterintuitive actions to remove all the fuel in one spot before the raging fire arrived was an untrained, counterintuitive strategy. He created a barren safety zone that the fire would bypass, leaving all within the circle unharmed. Unfortunately, his crew didn't see their future alive in that spot and chose to trust their own ability to outrun the fire. History tells the story of who won and who lost.

Counterintuitive moves are not always popular. In fact, most people don't even see them as reasonable but they are often necessary for survival. We must be willing to challenge our paradigms, even recognize that we may be suffering from the Dunning-Kruger Effect (see chap. 7).

Counterintuitive moves ... are often necessary for survival.

I had to do some work myself to organize this new way of thinking into a new paradigm. Six fundamental truths jumped out at me about movements and how they happen.

GOD-ORDAINED—MATTHEW 28:16–20

We must determine that having disciple-making disciples is the finish line—nothing less than a faith that replicates without a dependence on form, training, certification, ordination, or any other manmade heaviness that we've invented.

SPIRIT-DEPENDENT—MATTHEW 9:36–38

The harvest has been ready since Jesus' day. Movement-ready people are those who constantly and consistently express their dependence through prayer on the Father, the Spirit, and the Son. That constant connection with the Father develops a passion for those not yet in His family. Since there is no formula or human mechanism to make movements happen, we must consistently put the Father's eyes in our heart by asking Him to bring disciple-making disciples from the harvest.

BIBLE-CENTERED—2 TIMOTHY 3:16–17

Coming face to face with God is the primal, spiritually transforming experience. Jesus said, "My sheep *respond as they* hear My voice" (John 10:27), so our job is to get every people group's fingerprints on God's unshakable wisdom, the Bible. No source other than the Bible is trustworthy. Movement-ready people believe there is more power in reading and obeying the truth of God than in preaching or teaching the truth. The proclamation of the truth is providing pre-Christians the opportunity to hear from God by reading and obeying the Bible. This provides the potential growth effect of reaching every person on the planet.

OBEDIENCE-FOCUSED—JOHN 14:15

There is no other response to the Creator Redeemer God of the universe than to live in obedience to His divine wisdom. Movement-ready people have learned to put obedience at the front of every spiritual transformation. Through obedience to God's commands, we express our dependence on Him and acknowledge His wisdom above ours.

DISCOVERY-BASED—JOHN 6:44–45

God holds each of us accountable for our response to the truth. Our responsibility is to make sure everyone has a chance to read and obey the truth for themselves. Movement-ready people know that telling people what to believe is never as effective as helping them hear from God and decide for themselves if He is worthy of obeying.

DISCIPLE-DRIVEN—2 CORINTHIANS 5:16–21

Disciple-making disciples are God's intended strategy to take His good news to the ends of the earth. Movement-ready people shed all manmade heaviness to the good news and trust that God the Spirit is in control as ordinary people create small communities of obedience spreading the good news of God's reclaiming love to those who haven't a Father/child relationship with their Creator.

IT IS TIME TO JUMP!

I believe we are on a burning platform with an opportunity for a generation of Christian leaders to participate in a new Reformation or face the shame of spiritual irrelevancy.

We are on a burning platform.

If we continue to hold to this fixated mentality so many in the church have today, we will become like the Kodak executives who fought to remain faithful to their core business.

In the midst of this faithfulness, an employee invented the digital camera. Being alerted to the potential of digital photography and the disruption that it could bring, Kodak faithfully held tight to their core business. Thinking they could survive this disruption, they sought to gain market advantage by buying Sterling Drugs, only to discover that there is a big difference between chemicals and pharmaceuticals. Kodak ended up selling off Sterling Drugs in pieces for half the original purchase price not long after they purchased it.

Desperate to stay in the game, Kodak introduced the Advantix camera, a digital camera with film. It allowed a user to preview the picture before exposing the film. Holding fast to their core business while embracing the new proved a failure. They couldn't jump and hold on at the same time. To make a sad story short, in 2012 Kodak filed for bankruptcy. Its failure to jump into the digital world has been chronicled in numerous books and magazines.

We stand on the platform of historical methods that aren't necessarily wrong but have proven ineffective. But we hold to these methods. We count the passion of our grasp as a badge of biblical orthodoxy. Are we committed to a form rather than a function?

Jesus called us to disciple-making, not church planting! Churches are a means and not an end. Churches form as disciples obey all of Jesus' commands. We've injured the progress of the gospel by making an end a means and ignoring the means—disciple-making—altogether.

Permit me to use another business analogy. The LEGO company has undergone numerous changes in its history. LEGOs were first wood then became plastic after several warehouse fires that destroyed inventory. Plastic was not received well at first but slowly caught on and prevailed.

In the late 1960s Duplos were introduced to allow a younger population access to the creativity that the larger building blocks afforded. Instruction manuals, people with pose-able limbs, Legoland Parks, Technic and Model sets emerged as LEGO responded to the changing culture they operated in. LEGOs were traditionally red, white, yellow, blue, and black and were marketed to boys. When they appeared in pink and purple, LEGO expanded their appeal to a larger audience.

Unlike Kodak, LEGO was able to hold on to enduring functional principles rather than historical forms. Kodak could have been in the image business not the film and chemical business, but they fixated on forms and the result was financial insolvency. LEGO focused on functionality and endured the changes in markets.

If we jump from the platform we are on, I believe we can experience a new Reformation. Our current platform is fixed on forms rather than function. We have small building blocks of eternal truth that we can never give up. But when that truth is encased in forms that were never meant to have our undying allegiance, we fail to follow Jesus' last command, a command that encased a strategy that can permeate the very ends of the earth.

The good news of Jesus can be free from forms and spread without the heavy burdens that we've overloaded it with. It could be a new day for Christianity. Churches will sprout out of multiplicative

Disciple-Making Movements that bear the DNA of the Great Commission, churches where:

- disciple-making is primal in their psyche,

- obedience is the order of the day,

- the Bible stands as the source of truth and life so that Christ followers regularly have their fingerprints all over it.

We have examples of this happening in our world. They aren't Western. They are coming from the East, from cultures vastly different from the developed world. To grasp the opportunity in front of us will take some aggressive mental effort.

Effort that might often seem like the pain felt by Eustace, the boy become dragon in C. S. Lewis's *Voyage of the Dawn Treader*.

At the beginning of this book, nobody likes Eustace and for good reason. He is a nasty and selfish little boy. He boards Prince Caspian's ship with his cousins and they travel to the islands of Narnia. On one island Eustace stumbles into a cave to discover a mound of diamonds, rubies, and gold coins. He's beside himself with joy and imagines himself standing tall, finally getting what he deserves and showing all the others how superior he is to them. Confident of his plan he falls asleep. When he awakes he realizes he is in a dragon's cave, lying on the dragon's treasure and that he has become the dragon himself. Now, his ambitions are lost. His greed has turned him into a mean, ugly dragon, covered with a thick skin of hard, knobbly scales. His outer appearance now reflects the inner state of his heart.

Aslan, the Lion King of Narnia, arrives to rescue Eustace. He takes the boy-dragon to a pool in the forest and tells him to undress. Eustace discovers that the dragon skin comes off like a garment. He begins to rip and tear at the skin. But each time he scrapes off a layer of dragon skin, there is another one underneath. He does it again and again with the same result. Finally Eustace realizes that he is powerless to rid himself of the ugly dragon skin.

Later in the story Eustace describes the experience to his cousin, Edmond, who had a similar come-to-Jesus meeting in a previous story. "I was afraid of his claws . . . But I was pretty nearly desperate now. . . . Well, he peeled the beastly stuff right off—just as I thought I'd done it myself the other three times, only they hadn't hurt—and there it was lying on the grass: only ever so much thicker, and darker, and more knobby-looking than the others had been. Then he . . . threw me in the water. It smarted like anything but only for a moment. . . . And then I saw why. I'd turned into a boy again."[1]

It may take time and repeated effort as we tear off the layers of historically embedded cultural exegesis to see the true genius of our King and Savior. With a tenacity driven only by God the Spirit, we can arrive at a place that Jesus intended. He wanted us to discover the good news that has the potency to reach every culture on the earth.

For movements to take place in the West, we will need to have more mentally flexible leaders, people of influence who will challenge their paradigms and read the texts of the Bible unfiltered by theological frameworks and religious history that challenges their current mental models. It is a bimodal type of thinking, holding to some fundamental functionalities while remaining flexible with culture forms.

For movements of multiplicative disciple-making to emerge, soil has to be prepared. That soil consists of some clear understanding about movements and the mind shifts that take place to provide the seed bed for Disciple-Making Movements to erupt in the West.

I want to finish this book by collecting the ten mental movements or ten mind shifts necessary for movements to thrive in the twenty-first century. Some of these will be familiar. Remember, one of my educational principles is that people need to be reminded more than they need to be informed.

TEN MIND SHIFTS FOR MOVEMENTS TO EMERGE

1. FROM TRUSTING THE QUALIFIED TO RELEASING THE WILLING

The first and maybe most important is our view of the common man or woman (I prefer not to use *laypeople*). Most all of us will espouse a concept of the priesthood of the believer. Across the denominational and nondenominational landscape, concepts such as "every member a minister" are used to coax people out of the pew into the battle.

Theological statements such as "the ground at the foot of the cross is level" popularize the truth found in Galatians 3:28, where Paul declares there is no distinction among ethnicity, gender, or economic status for followers of Jesus. There is equality of access to God through the work of Jesus in this world.

But equality is not the practice. Despite all attempts to the contrary, the control-management mind-set is in operation all around us. Most of us grew up in homes where parents set the rules and made the decisions, and we went to schools where teachers and administrator were in charge. Our health care is delivered in such a fashion that we have little say in diagnosis or treatment. We go to work where we have bosses in charge who make most of the decisions. So it is only natural that, when it comes to designing organizations to further God's purposes in this world, we adopt the prevailing sentiments.

The plea to "let my people go" may find its origin in Moses' relationship with the pharaoh of Egypt, but a litany of books traversing almost every denomination have shouted this openly. Roland Allen, writing in the early 1900s, says that the movement of the good news "is hindered by a very widespread conviction that we cannot trust untrained men to propagate the Faith."[2] Allen stands in a long line of prophetic voices trying to remove the handcuffs from the common man and tap the greatest potential of the church.

Who is able to disciple? The trained, equipped, theologically educated, seminary graduate, and, of course, the ordained are. Why? Because we are stuck in the mental mind-set that presumes knowledge leads to spiritual maturity. This confounds me because some of the meanest, unloving people I know are chock full of Bible knowledge. Somehow it didn't work for them. The truth is, it doesn't work for everyone. It is not about knowledge but about obedience. Paul told us what knowledge does—it puffs us up (1 Cor. 13).

Until we give up our misplaced trust in subject-matter experts and understand that Jesus doesn't need the equipped but the willing, we will never mine the wealth of Christ followers and discover the viral power of the good news. As soon as someone begins to express obedience to Jesus, you have engaged a potential disciple-making disciple. All they need is a simple repeatable process to help others do the same thing they are doing so movements can begin.

It is not about knowledge but about obedience.

"But oh no, that couldn't happen!" many will say. But it did. We all are the result of it happening once. No seminaries or trained theologians, just ordinary people willing to obey Jesus. He started a Disciple-Making Movement with a team not even fully on board with who He was or what He was up to. He started anyway.

We fail to see that the gospel is the power of God, not a person's knowledge or character.

I can hear what you are thinking—He didn't have a choice, but we do. So you are saying that all-wise, powerful, and knowledgeable God painted Himself in a corner with the disciples he chose. He didn't have a choice? Surely you can see that you are defending your paradigm and not thinking clearly about God. He can do what He wants, when He wants, with whom He wants, right?

In *Why Nations Fail*, M.I.T economist Daron Acemoglu and Harvard political scientist James A. Robinson conclude that nations thrive when they develop inclusive political and economic institutions, and they fail when the institutions become "extractive" and concentrate power and opportunity in the hands of only a few.[3]

Maybe the church in the West is in trouble because we are exclusive. Is knowledge the currency of the exclusiveness that we have concentrated in the hands of the trained? Our confidence in the equipped has led to a sterile plateaued pattern of growth. We are like the cherry blossom trees in Washington DC. Everyone loves to look at them when they produce those soft pink blooms. They don't they produce cherries, only pretty flowers. They are ornamental rather than fruit producing, like many churches today.

In the mid-1800s underprivileged pregnant women in Vienna often gave birth in the street rather than using the services of the First Clinic at Vienna General Hospital. If they had to go to the hospital they requested the Second Clinic that was staffed by midwives rather than doctors.

Dr. Ignaz Semmelweis wondered why pregnant women would give birth in the street if they couldn't get into the Second Clinic when the First Clinic had space for them. He provided scientifically what the women know through word of mouth: the mortality rate among the doctors was one in ten, while the midwives held a much more successful ratio in one in fifty, despite the disparity in training.

Semmelweis changed the process for doctors and medical students in the hospital because the doctors were actually the cause of the mortality. Their medical education could not overcome the fact that they were bearers of what later became known as deadly germs (germ theory of disease had not yet been accepted) that led to the increase in mortality. They went from the Cadaver Lab where they had been participating in dissection to the maternity ward where they examined new mothers. What they took with them caused childbed fever, resulting in high mortality rates in patients in the First Clinic. At least half of those who developed the fever died. Rather than bringing healing those doctors were the bearers of death. Simply washing their hands produced a decrease in the mortality rate from one in ten to one in one hundred.[4]

Christian leaders need to radically and ruthlessly reexamine the faulty theological frameworks built through centuries of misreading the Bible. Movements of multiplicative disciple-making don't happen in an atmosphere of hierarchal exclusivity. People movements throughout history have happened when people's bias for action is not stymied by wondering if they have permission or if they are qualified. God the Father is in our world reconciling it to Himself (2 Cor. 5:16–21) and ready to be the Teacher (John 6:44–46). God the Spirit is ready to lead people to God the Son (John 16:8–11). It is time to "let the people go" by giving them a simple, repeatable strategy for making disciple-making disciples.

2. FROM MAKING DISCIPLES TO MAKING DISCIPLE-MAKING DISCIPLES

This isn't just a play on words; it's a shift from selfish, me-centered approaches to spreading the good news to a submission of our methods to the last command of Jesus. When we come to believe that Jesus called us to equip people to make disciples, we catch the replicating nature of the Great Commission. If our disciples can't make disciples, we fail to obey Jesus.

Making disciple-making disciples demands that our methodologies are submissive to the Great Commission. Rather than making disciples out of our giftedness, passions, and personalities, we must make disciples with simple and repeatable methodologies that can be used by everyone.

3. FROM HUMAN REPRODUCTION TO VIRAL REPLICATION

Our mental models can control our intake of information and affect how we put truth into practice. For centuries, the paradigm of human reproduction has controlled our understanding of disciple-making. From infancy through childhood, humans can't reproduce, but once adolescence is reached reproduction is possible. The metaphor of reproduction has forced us into thinking in terms of the time it takes for humans to reproduce. We automatically assume it takes the same amount of time to reproduce in the spiritual world.

This picture of spiritual infancy to childhood to adult holds the Great Commission captive. One cannot reproduce until they grow from infancy to adulthood. Coupled with an addiction to content-driven disciple-making, these two errant ideas keep us from see-ing the true nature of Jesus' last command. Although a person may grow in her understanding of the Creator God and His great work in this world, there is no biblical reason to press the pause button on the disciple-making process for this to take place. The maturation process will take place for all eternity as we grasp, from our finite nature, the infinite nature of our Father in heaven. Once again, we confuse ends and means. Disciple-making is the means, and spiritual growth is the end. We disciple so people can grow; we don't grow them so they can disciple.

There is nothing of human reproduction in the Great Commis-sion. It resembles more of a viral replication. Many viruses are most potent near the transfer from one organism to another. The longer you wait the more likely the host organism is to fight the infection and render it nontransferable. In Matthew 28, Jesus lays out a viral replication metaphor for us to follow: "Identify them with my cause and teach them to obey." Simple, repeatable. Disciple-making is not about the accumulation of content but the submission of will.

It is biblical but counterintuitive for us to think that once people start obeying Jesus they could actually be a part of discipling others. I know that their hearts are inclined to believe that what they are learning about Jesus matters more than anything else. If a simple, repeatable process is used to help them begin obeying Jesus' command, they can use the same process in their relational networks to spread the good news by discipling their friends, relatives, neighbors, and workmates. In turn, they create a viral movement of the good news that spreads unimpeded by forms.

4. FROM FORM TO FUNCTION
(PLANTING CHURCHES TO MAKING DISCIPLE-MAKING DISCIPLES)

Jesus said, "I will build my church" (Matthew 16:19).
Jesus said, "Go, make disciples" (Matthew 28:19).

Paul heard Him loud and clear and taught his disciple Timothy the same. "And the things you have heard me say in the presence of many witnesses entrust to reliable men who will also be qualified to teach others" (2 Tim. 2:2 NIV).

Our role is not to get wrapped up with organizational forms that promote the spread of the gospel but to call people into obedience based a relationship to Jesus. He promised that He would build His church. History has proven that when Christians make disciples churches are built, but when we plant churches we don't always get disciples.

5. FROM CONVERSION TO MAKING DISCIPLES

Although persuasive evangelism might be effective in some cultures, in many Western contexts as well as other highly religious cultures it has difficulties. It certainly is not the biblical standard and should not be considered the standard approach to spreading the good news.

The twenty-first century is littered with people who trust in a prayer they prayed or with the comfort that they have "accepted," when in fact they may not understand the good news that Jesus brought. To demand allegiance without addressing the will, without teaching to obey, is to attempt to spread the good news in a way that is foreign to Jesus.

6. FROM INDIVIDUALS TO GROUPS

In Luke 10, Jesus trained His disciples to find a household receptive to the faith and stay put. This is known as the "person of peace" principle. Jesus' intent was to plant the good news in existing relational networks and let it run free. Of the thirty gospel encounters in Acts, only three are individual. Simple, repeatable disciple-making strategies make it possible for an outsider to find an inside person of peace, begin the disciple-making process with this person, and coach the progress through the social network.

7. FROM KNOWLEDGE FOCUSED (TRANSFER OF CONTENT) TO OBEDIENCE FOCUSED (TRANSFORMATIONAL EXPERIENCES)

Our Western traditions have polluted the stream of disciple-making. Knowledge has played a pivotal role in the economic development of the West. As such it has infiltrated modern Christianity to the point that most of our disciple-making activities consist of knowledge transfer rather than obedience teaching. It is as if we heard Jesus say "teach them all things" rather than "teach them to obey all things." In accordance with the Great Commission our efforts should be aimed at designing learning experiences that equip people to obey all of Jesus' wisdom.

8. FROM THINKING LIKE A MARKETER
TO THINKING LIKE A REVOLUTIONARY

Church today is often described as a program-driven organization. There is nothing inherently evil with an organization. In fact all organisms have organization. The Creator God brought order out of chaos in creating the world.

Our concern shouldn't be to abandon the organization but to learn how to influence it. Programs come and go in the West; therefore, they have to be refreshed constantly. But changing a culture via its DNA changes it for a lifetime. Marketers deal with programs (forms); revolutionaries focus on DNA (functions). Marketers focus on tactics while revolutionaries develop strategies. Tossing out our old ways of thinking and being willing to work with a few holy dissatisfied saints gives us the chance to embed movement DNA. It might be slower but it has greater potential.

9. FROM LEADING TOWARD TO LEADING FROM

Reformation requires a new kind of leader. Brian Eno, an Ambient music composer, says of Ambient music that it must be ignored to be engaged.[5] That seems a strange statement from someone who creates music. However, he understands that his style of music is made to be in the background.

Movements need leaders who understand how to influence in the background. They don't move with a sense of personal power and vocal influence. Their power is not seen or felt in traditional ways; therefore, it doesn't create dependence. Their presence is not needed for the good news to keep moving. Their influence comes in connecting people to the Bible and God rather than to themselves. They know how to disappear, work behind the scenes, play a lesser role, and avoid credit for God's work.

10. FROM BEING A CONTENT PROVIDER TO BEING A LEARNING DESIGNER

This new Reformation needs leaders who have patience for people to discover the truth rather than taking shortcuts to tell them what they are looking for. In this trained and equipped world, emotional maturity is required to stop using vocal power and mental knowledge. Movement catalysts focus on simple repeatable processes, the DNA of movements.

Movement catalysts understand that doing is the preferred style of learning, not listening. They eagerly design learning environments for people rather than display their grasp of content. They are not eager to display their knowledge or answer questions. They understand that teaching means to help people make meaning of God's truth in their reality.

APPENDIX A

FACILITATION GUIDE

SUGGESTED TIME: 10–15 MINUTES

1. Review (Key DNA #1 Accountability)

   - How did you do with last week's "I will" and sharing?

   - With whom did you share last week's lesson?

   - How did you put into practice what you learned from last week's lesson?

SUGGESTED TIME: 20 MINUTES

2. What are you thankful for this week? (Key DNA #2)

3. What is stressing you out lately? (Key DNA #3)

4. Do you have a need or know anyone with a need that this group can meet? (Key DNA #4)

SUGGESTED TIME: 35 MINUTES

5. What is God saying? (Key DNA #5)

   Refer to Scripture list to find the passage for today.

   - Read the designated passage aloud in two different versions, if available.

   - Ask someone to be prepared to retell the passage in his or her own words.

   - Have the appointed person retell the passage.

   - Ask others to help add to what may have been missed or their insights

- Use the LEMON BITE (see Note 3 on page 208) questions, if groups needs help discussing the passage.

SUGGESTED TIME: 20 MINUTES

6. If this is God speaking, what will I do? (Key DNA #6)

- Develop a tangible statement that will put into practice what you learned from the designated passage. For example, "I will take ten minutes per day to reflect on how much God loves me," or "I will begin to recycle because God has given me the earth to take care of."

- To develop good "I will" statements, you might need to take a few minutes of silence to let each person think and reflect. Then ask someone to share what they have developed.

- Work to get each "I will" statement specific, measurable, achievable, realistic, and time-bound (SMART).

- Make sure someone records the "I will" statements so you can ask about them next week.

SUGGESTED TIME: 5 MINUTES

7. With whom will you share what you learned this week? (Key DNA #7)

- Share with at least one person preferably who is not in a relationship with God and preferably someone already in your relational network.

SUGGESTED TIME: 5 MINUTES

Follow-up (This may have been accomplished when you asked question #4)

- Are there actionable things that can be done?
- How can the group meet these needs?

◎ Where are we meeting next week?

FACILITATION GUIDELINES

◎ Don't allow one person to teach or explain.

◎ A good facilitator doesn't give answers, but asks questions.

◎ Give everyone a chance to share even if you have to call on people to share.

◎ Don't just read the passages; put them into practice. Obedience is the goal!

◎ Share with other people what you are learning about your life with God.

◎ Meet practical needs in the group and in the community.

◎ After week two, someone besides you should be facilitating the group. Then pass the facilitation around the group. With only seven questions to ask, facilitating is easy.

NOTE 1: NO TEACHING OR EXPLAINING.

Ask questions; let people find answers in the Bible. How do I know when I am teaching or explaining in a Discovery Group?

◎ I hear the sound of my voice more than the others.

◎ People do not interrupt me (I Cor. 14:30).

◎ After I have spoken, the group goes silent.

◎ I share prior knowledge rather than revelation from the Word in the moment.

◎ I am more concerned with correcting others than I am about them hearing from God.

◎ The members of the group are receiving truth from me and not the Bible.

- I participate in the discussion, but struggle to make and keep obedience statements.

- I find it easy to apply the Bible to the mistakes of others, but difficult to apply the Bible to correct my own lifestyle.

NOTE 2: NO BRINGING IN OTHER PASSAGES.

Those not familiar with the Bible will feel uncomfortable if people bounce around the Bible.

- Focus on the one central truth in the passage.

- Use the question, "How do you get that from this passage?" as a segue back to the passage when group members express opinions or try to bring in other passages.

NOTE 3: LEMON BITE

A memory aid to help stimulate discussion and get to the point of the passage A (attention) Lemon (like) Bite (bother) Gathers (God) Many (mankind) Looks (life).

These help with discovering the passage's meaning:

- A - Did anything in this passage capture your **attention**?

- L - What did you **like** about this passage?

- B - Did anything **bother** you? Why?

These help with getting to what God is saying to me:

- G - What does this passage tell us about **God**?

- M - What does this passage tell us about **mankind**?

- L - What does this passage tell us about the **life** God desires for us?

APPENDIX B

THREE-COLUMN METHOD OF BIBLE STUDY

Discovering God is a lifelong pursuit. Along this journey, several practices will be vital to growing your faith and becoming a fully devoted follower of Jesus Christ. One of the most important spiritual movements you can engage in is to regularly and consistently relate to God through His Word, the Bible.

People often overcomplicate reading the Bible. To assist you in discovering and implementing this spiritual discipline, a simple process is given below to help you interact with the Bible and get the most out of your time relating to God through His Word.

Turn a sheet of blank paper sideways and make three columns like the picture below. Label the first Scripture, the second My Words and the third I Will Do & Share.

Scripture	My Words	I Will Do & Share

1. Write the passage word-for-word in the first column.

2. Write the passage in your own words in the second column.

3. Ask God to reveal something you need to add to your life, take away from your life, or change in your life to obey this passage. Write your "I Will" statement in the third column along with the person you plan to share it with.

Grab a Bible and give it a try. This is a discipline you will want to continue throughout your spiritual journey. If you desire, continue reading for a much more detailed explanation of this three-step way to study the Bible.

THREE-COLUMN STUDY DETAILS

SCRIPTURE

When you copy a passage word-for-word, you actually read it through several (about five–seven) times. It is a form of forced meditation for those of us who can't sit and think about a passage without losing focus. This process also keeps you from skimming familiar passages. When you write it out, you have to think about every word.

MY WORDS

After writing the passage word-for-word, use the second column to write the passage in your own words. Write it as if you're telling a friend about it over coffee. Don't move on until you can write the passage in your own words. You see, you don't really understand it if you can't tell it to someone in your own words. And you can't obey Scripture unless you understand it. It's that simple. Sometimes you will have to stop on a passage, read it again, and think about it quite a bit before you can put it in your own words. Often you won't believe how much you know and yet how little you understand.

I WILL

In the third column, you transition from knowing God's Word to obeying God's Word. Look at each part of the passage and ask God to reveal things you need to add to your life, take away from your life, or change in your life for you to obey this passage. Be very specific. The passage may say that God created the earth, but you have to decide what that means in your life. How does your life change because you believe that God created the earth?

What do you need to do differently? What can you do in the next twenty-four to forty-eight hours to obey this passage? Every time we open God's Word, He invites us into relationship. We call His invitation *grace* because we can't do anything to deserve it. Obedience is how we accept His invitation. God lives with those who obey His Word (John 14:23–24). When we study God's Word, we have a choice: we choose to obey Him or we choose to disobey Him. It is really that simple. See this third column as your response to God's invitation.

SHARE

As you complete the three-column study, you have two responsibilities. First, you need to meet with other followers of Christ in your relational circles and discuss what you learned. You need to tell them your "I Will" statements and ask them to hold you accountable as they figure out ways to help you obey God's Word. Second, look for opportunities to share what God said to you. Try to work the phrase, "God taught me something today," or something similar, into your conversation and wait for the other person's response. This creates discussion opportunities. If people are interested, they ask for more information. If it isn't the right time for them, they ignore you, and you don't continue to share. When they do ask, share what God taught you, and if it's the right time, they will ask more questions. Their questions help you understand where they are in their spiritual journeys. You don't want to move faster than the Holy Spirit wants you to, or you risk pushing them away from the gospel.

APPENDIX C

WHAT THE FUTURE
COULD LOOK LIKE

Josh and Jordanne Wilkes started attending Shoal Creek three years ago when their first child was born. Jordanne grew up nominally Methodist, and Josh was raised Catholic. Neither had a real affinity for their religious pedigree, but both knew that they wanted a spiritual influence in their lives but not a church.

After seven months of Sundays they decided to jump into a group. Their first group came after hearing a series on relationships and that God created us to live in relationship with others. Josh looked at Jordanne and said, "I can stand anything for a few weeks." Off they went to a house full of strangers yet found the environment to be stimulating. It didn't take long for strangers to become friends.

They were surprised that no one taught the group, but they also were amazed that for the first time they were looking at the Bible for themselves. Each week's discussion centered around a different part of the Bible. The facilitators actually didn't seem to know that much about the Bible or at least they didn't overwhelm anyone with their knowledge if they did.

After the second week Josh admitted that they didn't even own a Bible. Their group facilitator met Josh at Outfitters on Sunday and helped him pick out the Wilkes's first Bible. Josh felt a bit trapped. Now that he owned a Bible people were going to expect him to read it.

By the third week both Josh and Jordanne found themselves talking about these "I will" statements that each group member developed. They both found a freedom in the group focusing on doing what the Bible says rather than having to know a lot about the Bible.

As the weeks passed Josh knew that thirteen weeks was not enough. He enjoyed the discussion and found himself cracking open the Bible at home. He knew something was going on, and he wanted to chase this thing further. If only his fraternity brothers could see him now.

Josh had seen some changes in Jordanne and was hopeful that she might feel the same. Their discussions about their relationship were deeper and more sensitive than ever. Both felt an eerie sense of something moving that they couldn't explain. And they agreed that there was more.

When their group facilitator suggested that they might want to continue with the next set of Bible passages, they were hooked. Though they wondered how another group commitment would work with Josh's softball league and Jordanne's job that often demanded long hours, the mysterious and deep things they were feeling made it almost impossible to say no.

Although they had only been with these people for three months, they really wanted some of them to join them on the next stage. That caused Josh to speak up even before talking with Jordanne and suggest the group join them. Not everyone had the same interest level that Josh and Jordanne had but a few others did.

Three weeks later they found themselves in a new group with one couple from their former group members with them. They had a sense of anticipation because they had heard the 7 Journeys mentioned many times from the stage on Sunday morning.

Learning to trust God as they moved from earner to heir in their relationship with Him was life changing for the Wilkes. More than once they joked about the rainbow-colored hair guy at the Chiefs game that had the 3XL T-shirt that said "John 3:16." Jordanne had to tell Josh that it was a reference to the Bible! The study brought a meaning to "God so loved the world" that was life changing for the Wilkes. The idea of living in God's favor because of Jesus dying on the cross took a hold of the Wilkeses.

As they were finishing the second stage of their group, the Wilkeses had the Cornwallises over to watch the Chiefs on *Monday Night Football*. Sara Cornwallis was sharing with Jordanne some of the difficulties that she and her husband, Bill, were having in their marriage. Without really thinking, Jordanne began talking about the difference that she and Josh had been experiencing because they were in this group that looked to the Bible for answers.

Sara thought that sounded a bit old-fashioned and said so. Jordanne agreed that she thought the same thing until she actually started reading the Bible for herself. Sara then complained that the Bible was hard to understand, but Jordanne challenged her gently, "Have you ever read it?" Sara's bluff was called; she had never even opened a Bible.

That night lying in bed Sara mentioned the conversation to Bill. He was intrigued that a couple like Josh and Jordanne might be Bible thumpers and drilled Sara for every detail of the conversation.

Josh and Bill were scheduled to play golf the following Saturday. On the third hole Bill asked Josh about this group that Jordanne had mentioned to Sara. Josh could see that Bill was more than inquisitive. Fifteen holes later Josh asked Bill if he and Sara would be interested in joining their group. Josh knew that this would be a huge step for the Cornwallises and an even bigger step for the Wilkeses.

While waiting for an answer from Bill and Sara, the Wilkeses talked to their group facilitator about the possibility of a new couple joining their group. Their facilitator was more than excited and assured Josh and Jordanne that he would walk beside them as they built this relationship with the Cornwallises.

But then their group facilitator threw a curve ball at Josh and Jordanne: How would they feel about facilitating a new group that the Cornwallises could join instead of growing the group they were in? The Wilkeses had been thinking they would bring the Cornwallises into their existing group. The Croziers, their group facilitators, explained to them that this wouldn't be a good idea.

If the Cornwallises simply joined in with the already established group, they would start in the middle and not at the beginning where the Wilkeses got a chance to start; besides, adding more people to the group was going to make it much harder to keep the group to two hours, which was a struggle with the current numbers.

The Croziers assured the Wilkeses that they could easily facilitate the process that they had been experiencing for the past six months. In fact they reminded them they had facilitated the group several times and lived to tell about it. They would simply be doing what they have already experienced in their group.

The Croziers were careful not to set themselves up as subject-matter experts. Regularly they would take questions they were asked and drive people back to the Bible to find the answers for themselves. It took everything in them not to give the answers, but they had become convinced that the easy way, just answering questions, stunted everyone's spiritual growth.

The Croziers not only were reassuring but also upped the ante! They suggested that Josh and Jordanne use this as an opportunity to invite several people into a new group since several had dropped out. All the while raising the Wilkeses sights, the Croziers also explained that they would be there every step of the way, even present in their group if they needed them. But neither the Wilkeses nor Croziers thought that would be necessary.

In the middle of the week, Sara called Jordanne and told her that she and Bill might be interested. Jordanne assured her that she understood their hesitancy. In the midst of this discussion, Jordanne asked Sara if she thought Vince and Sue Voight would be interested. Sara was surprised and somewhat excited about the thought. She and Bill wouldn't be the only "newbies" in the group. Sara and Sue were best friends and Vince and Bill worked in IT at the same company. It didn't take much convincing for Sara to ask Sue and Vince to join them.

Come to find out, Vince and Sue were interested. Vince grew up in a Jewish family that really didn't practice or adhere to much of anything, and Sue's family just never got around to religion. They both often wondered why people even went to church. Yet they had turned thirty a few years ago and were feeling a sense of loss as they asked the question, "Is this all there is?"

After spending six months in two different groups, Josh and Jordanne found themselves leading a group made up of the Cornwallises and Voights, with Jim and Sally Crozier, their group facilitators, shadowing them for support.

Jim and Sally had been following Christ for fifteen years. They were early adopters of the Shoal Creek strategy. In the past few years their excitement for their spiritual journey seemed to wane. They served, gave, and read their Bibles, but something was missing.

When the discovery process and the "Go" strategy were engaged, they looked at it with skepticism. However, they had always been good soldiers, so they learned all they could about the process and strategy and volunteered to help lead. Little did they know the pure adrenaline their souls would feel when they volunteered. Their very first group was a Bridge Group using Bible passages on marriage. Most of the people who came had been around Shoal Creek for a while so the discussions were predictable. When it ended after four weeks they were even more skeptical.

Since they had read the study guides provided by Shoal Creek, the 7 Journeys meant a great deal to them personally, so once again they volunteered to lead in the new semester-based approach to groups. By the fifth week of this group, they were hooked. Sitting in their living room with people who had never opened the Bible and yet were willing to open their hearts to a spiritual journey stoked their fire big time!

Now they were experiencing even greater sense of purpose because one of the couples in their group stumbled into starting a group and they were going to be able to practice the Mentor, Assist, Watch, and Leave (MAWL) process they had learned.

The first week of the Wilkes's group was spent getting to know one another better and filling in the holes they had missed over the couple of years they had known one another. Both the Cornwallises and Voights had their doubts but were secretly excited to see where this might lead!

Josh and Jordanne were straightforward and talked about their experiences reading the Bible. They let everyone know that through personally reading the Bible and finding out what God has to say about life, their lives and marriage had been changed. They had starting letting Jesus be their sole consultant about life and that was what had changed them. This group was about hearing from God through the Bible, they told everyone, not about getting them to go to church.

The next two weeks were full of discussion disagreements and more questions than time would allow. Josh and Jordanne knew that the group time would really be key since the couples would have a chance to open the Bible for themselves. And open the Bible they did. It was eye opening for Josh and Jordanne to hear their neighbors this way. If everyone else on the block could hear this discussion the neighborhood would be aflame!

The Croziers continued to meet, call, and provide encouragement to Josh and Jordanne so they were not on their own. All the couples wanted to continue meeting after they had finished the series of passages on Earner to Heir—Trust, which surprised the Wilkeses. It was clear that Sue, Bill, and Vince were really getting it but Sara seemed a bit confused or maybe even resistant. It was hard for her to understand that she wasn't a "good" person.

It was in Journey 3, moving from Receiver to Giver, that Vince seemed to light up spiritually. It created some tension between Sue, who was still struggling, and himself. Vince seemed to irritate Sue because he felt he knew the cause—Sue's fear of having to give up her love of nice things.

Vince had been sharing what he was learning with a couple of guys at work. Being IT guys they kind of took a scientific approach to spirituality. In talking with Josh about it, he decided he would test their interest by offering to host a group at work over lunch once a week. Once his coworkers understood the idea of a Discovery Group, they agreed. Josh suggested Vince think out loud to other coworkers and see who all might want to join. Sure enough two more guys did.

At lunch on Tuesday of the next week Vince scheduled a conference room for them to meet in—five guys with their lunches around a table. Two had pretty extensive church background, one grew up Catholic and another Baptist, while the other two claimed to be pretty clueless about the Bible, God, and Jesus but were eager to learn more. They started in Genesis and began a weekly journey together.

Josh and Jordanne talked regularly with the Croziers about the group and their own personal journeys. During one of these discussions, the Wilkeses were challenged to attend the Tuesday/Thursday facilitators group. Jim and Sally believed that the Wilkeses needed a place to come and share their lives with other facilitators. When Jim mentioned it was at 5:30 a.m. Jordanne went into cardiac arrest. She hadn't been up at that time since her bachelorette party and that was a mistake she would like to forget.

Jim and Sally simply asked them to give it a try. If the support group added to their lives, they could make it a habit; if not, then they could forget about it. Sally shared how the investment of her time in this group had become a habit that she wouldn't miss despite a busy lifestyle.

The Croziers advice had always proved valuable to Josh and Jordanne and this was no exception. The energy of being around others involved in the same mission was rewarding. Listening and learning for others made the trouble it took to carve time in their schedule well worth it. These meetings gave them the patience they needed to continue with their group.

When The Wilkeses attended their first facilitators' gathering, their eyes were opened to what was happening. Little did they know that so many groups were in play in this part of the city. They heard reports for existing initiatives in workplaces. Several major employers in the area had ten to forty groups going. There was even a structure that supported the facilitators of these groups that met regularly at the workplace. The same was true for those working in the neighborhood.

It was exciting to hear people who were praying about starting work in different groups, like parents whose children play on competitive sports teams, among growing Hispanic and Chinese populations, international students at colleges, and the homeless.

They were introduced to a whole new vocabulary. *Outside facilitator* was a term being used for those seeking to enter a particular population and they were seeking to build Access ministries, or activities that give a person a legitimate reason to be present in a neighborhood, workplace, or group. They discovered that they were *inside facilitators* since they were working with their neighbors. The word most used was *movement.* Even though they were newbies they felt compelled to ask for a definition.

They got more than they bargained for: a movement, others explained, was an intentional, divinely empowered, disciple-making expansion of the church in a neighborhood, region, or group, resulting in an increase in the number of disciples (baptisms) and disciplers (groups self-propagating), causing a widespread increase in disciples engaging with needs in their community and significant and spontaneous multiplication of churches/groups or spiritual communities.

A locally based international software company was used as an example of developing *inside facilitators.* Before and after work and at lunch, people from Shoal Creek offered multiple training sessions to teach interested employees how to lead the discovery process—a simple, repeatable outline for leading people to discover who God is, why Jesus came, and how they can connect with them.

The Wilkeses' first meeting was filled with all kinds of Ahas! They now understood the whys behind the whats of the groups they had been in and the one they were now leading. Josh was late to work because he couldn't stop talking with Jordanne about all that they had learned. While on his way to work he looked at the cars around him and wondered who might be in a Discovery Group somewhere and walked into work with a whole different vision for what might be, at work!

As a couple of years passed, Josh and Jordanne saw some amazing work of God in their neighborhood. Much of it happened beyond arm's reach for them. Vince caught fire both at work and in the neighborhood. He loved the discovery process and had a knack for inviting people in. Personally he had started six groups and two of those groups gave birth to a dozen more.

Over three years the Wilkeses could count sixty groups started in their subdivision and well over seventy-five baptized active disciple-makers. Now they were leading the facilitators groups. Their role moved from facilitator to mentor/movement catalyst. They even have a neighborhood gathering at the club-house once a month where they sing together and take Communion and baptize people who are ready to make their faith public.

They don't attend Shoal Creek as religiously as they once did, but the movement-building spirit at Shoal Creek gives them fuel for their fire. Some of the people in the subdivision attend Shoal Creek, but the majority consider what is happening in their subdivision as their church. The story continues.

RESOURCES FOR THE JOURNEY

RESOURCES

DGapp.org (a webapp for use in facilitating a Discovery Group). Watch for Android app in fall of 2015

DiscoverDMM.com—a place to start your learning process

MakeDisciples.US—explore the numbers surrounding the expansion of Christianity

CityTeam.org

AccelerateTeams.org

ContagiousDisciplemaking.com

Engage! is an interactive course designed to give churches and individuals experience in expanding and extending God's Kingdom by facilitating Discovery Bible Studies (DBS) and initiating a Disciple-Making Movement (DMM). For more information contact: jking@finalcommand.org

BOOKS AND ARTICLES

Roland Allen. *The Spontaneous Expansion of the Church and the Causes that Hinder It* (Eugene, OR: Wipf and Stock Publishers, 1962).

David Watson and Paul Watson. *Contagious Disciple-Making* (Nashville: Thomas Nelson, 2014).

Jerry Trousdale. *Miraculous Movements* (Nashville: Thomas Nelson, 2012).

Patrick Robertson and David Watson. *Father Glorified* (Nashville: Thomas Nelson, 2013).

Ted Esler. "Two Church Planting Paradigms." *International Journal of Frontier Missiology*, Summer 2013.

Dave Hunt. *A Revolution in Church Multiplication in East Africa: Transformational Leaders Develop A Self-Sustainable Model of Rapid Church Multiplication*, dissertation submitted to the faculty of Bakke University in candidacy for degree of doctor of ministry.

COACHING

Starting a Disciple-Making Movements Learning Community (DMLC).

Gather a group for two hours for nine weeks to explore the ten mind-shifts needed to get from ministry to movement. Contact Roy Moran (roy.moran@shoalcreek.org).

ACKNOWLEDGMENTS

This book is a result of connections. If you know me, you are probably in one of the streams of connection. I wish I could be complete, but space confines me to mention just a few.

Fathers are the fire starters of great accomplishments. I am blessed beyond measure to have a father, Ed Moran, who loved me no matter what. His constant faith and abiding love provided the soil in which God has been at work.

While sitting around the kitchen table at Dick and Ann Abel's, I met Jay Lorenzen, who turned me on to Cru at Baylor University. The Christmas of my freshmen year at a Cru conference I heard Howard G. Hendricks and decided at that moment I wanted his influence in my life. Although many professors impacted my life, none did so more than Prof (a term of endearment used for Howard Hendricks among the Dallas Seminary tribe). My four years at Dallas Seminary found me lurking outside Prof's door. I poached whatever time I could so that his influence leaked deep into my psyche. He taught me to think differently.

Sid Buzzell, my thesis adviser, suggested I consider writing my thesis in an area that would allow me to interact with Ted Ward. That was like pouring gasoline on a fire! Dr. Ted Ward's point of view altered my understanding of human interaction, especially his concept of leadership.

I spent hours listening to and reading anything I could get my hands on by David Watson. Then a guest post on David Watson's blog led to a request of David Broodryk to lead a workshop on disciple-making while in Africa. David Broodryk arranged for me to get an invite to Cityteam International's Global Leadership Conference. Patrick Robertson and Cityteam opened their minds and hearts to me. They have messed me up in the most amazing ways, from which I will never recover.

At a chance meeting over lunch at a Willow Creek Roundtable at Heartland Community Church, I was seated next to Glenn Kahler. A week later I was back around a table with Glenn and Craig McElvain, and months later I found myself at Willow Creek Community Church for a conference, where I heard Bill Hybels for the first time. His irrational passion for people far from God ruined me for any kind of normal life. Bill and the team at Willow gave me the courage to advocate creatively, relentlessly, and unashamedly for the spiritually disenfranchised. Mac, Glen, and the Heartland Community Church crowd nurtured Shoal Creek into existence.

While working for the Fellowship of Christian Athletes (FCA), I begged a friend at Zondervan to give me some free books for the FCA staff. He sent me *The Spirit of the Disciplines* by Dallas Willard. My relationship with Dallas was not an easy one. No one has ever challenged my ability to think as he did. From *The Spirit of the Disciplines* to *Divine Conspiracy*, I spent many hours reading and rereading trying to get my little brain around Willard's elephantine explanation of Jesus. Somehow Dallas walked me from the complex to the simple. I am forever grateful for Dallas showing me that there is a simplicity that exists on the other side of complexity.

While sitting in a pantry area of my home, in a deep depression after being fired from my job at FCA, I aimlessly roamed through the boxes that now housed my library. Larry Crabb's *Understanding People* chose me. In a deep darkness, I traipsed through it and *Effective Biblical Counseling, Inside Out, Silence of Adam,* and eventually everything Larry penned. Larry taught me how to live in the darkness and find the God who would and could transform me there. I learned from Larry to love the darkness.

As she sat in the left field bleachers in Willow Creek's old auditorium, my wife, Candy Moran, prophesied to me. Bill Hybels had just finished exposing his soul, advocating for churches built for those far from God. Candy turned to me and said, "I think you can do this!" I am not fond of what we call "the church." Not that I have a tragic story in my past where mean church people screwed me over. I've just always known that there is very little flexibility in the forms we've chosen. Candy's comment on top of Hybels's plea was the catalyst to send us on a journey that led to Shoal Creek. She is a prophetess, creative muse, constant encourager, and consummate servant of whatever needs to be done. Without Candy, there would be no words in this book.

My children have lived a life in tow of an ecclesiastical entrepreneur. Living in a family on mission meant they didn't have the cars, game systems, or name-brand clothes their friends had. They did have a front row seat to eternity, watching many lives change in front of their eyes. As a father, I live with knowledge that I have injured them in ways only time will tell. Their willingness to come along on this journey is a gift I will treasure to my grave. Alyssa, Trevor, Jessie, and Colin partnered with us in living out this crazy dream, and I hope that we are all the better for it.

So many people have gone over the cliff with me on this journey. It is what continues to convince me that God is in the house. Candy, Jason, Rachel, Trevor, Justin, Sean, Eric, Derek, and Shea have hitched their families' livelihoods to this vision. Some raising their own support, others taking massive pay cuts to be all in. Their gifts and partnership shaped, supported, and taught me every step of the way.

I couldn't write these words if hundreds of spiritually interested people hadn't found their way into our relational networks and patiently endured our experimentation with spiritual truths. Watching them burst into a new life, living in the favor of their newfound Father was and is the fuel that keeps us going. For those early years of survival, I am grateful to the many who served, gave, and shared their spiritual journeys with friends, neighbors, and workmates.

Thanks to all who call Shoal Creek home. You having given me hope in this world as you respond to the truth. You are my inspiration.

For the better part of ten years, Shoal Creek ran an internship. As many as twenty college students would descend on us for twelve weeks. The men lived in my basement and the women in a carriage house on my property. Their presence each summer sharpened my thinking and kept me young. Many of their stories are still being lived out at Shoal Creek. Ben Koehn, a shy, self-deprecating lad from small-town Missouri was one of those. Ben's literary genius has yet to be discovered, but his marketing prowess has already emerged. He came up with *Spent Matches* as a title. Thanks, Ben, and I can't wait to read your first book!

A trip to Nashville to visit a coconspirator in disciple-making strategies, John King, led to a chance meeting with Frank Couch. Two and a half hours later this project had begun. I am grateful to these two for forcing me to put on paper what I've been thinking and living out.

No one will ever know the horror that I am sure Alee Anderson felt the day this manuscript appeared in her inbox. Thomas Nelson probably doesn't pay enough for the miracle that she and Maleah Bell have performed in turning what they were given into a publishable work.

Though the words and thoughts in this book are inspired by many, the responsibility for their formulation is my responsibility. If you are going to draw and quarter anyone, let it be me. My hope is not that you agree with me but that you engage the discussion of a new Reformation. It is my hope that in my lifetime the last command of Jesus will be the driving force of what we call The Church. May the bride of Christ become passionate about and obedient to its founder's last command, The Great Commission.

NOTES

CHAPTER 1

1. Jim Collins, *Good to Great: Why Some Companies Make the Leap . . . And Others Don't* (New York: HarperBusiness; 2001), 85.

2. Joel Arthur Barker, *Paradigms: The Business of Discovering the Future* (New York: HarperBusiness, 1993), 15.

3. Ibid, 15–19, 144, 149.

4. Patrick Johnstone, *The Future of the Global Church* (Milton Keynes, UK: Authentic Media Limited, 2011).

5. Bradley A. Coon. "One Hundred Years of Christian Growth," *Lusanne World Pulse* April 2007, 2.

6. Todd M. Johnson, Peter F. Crossing, and Bobby Jangsun Ryu, "Looking Forward: An Overview of World Evangelization, 2005–2025. A special report for the Lausanne 2004 Forum on World Evangelization Center for the Study of Global Christianity, Gordon-Conwell Theological Seminary," 2.

7. "Christianity by 2014: Independent Christianity and Slum Dwellers," Center for the Study of Global Christianity, January 2014, 29.

8. David Barrett and Todd Johnson, *World Christian Trends* (Pasadena: William Carey Library, 2001), 841.

9. Roland Allen, *The Spontaneous Expansion of the Church* (Eugene, OR: Wipf & Stock Publishers, 1997), 22.

10. Todd M. Johnson et al., "Christianity in its Global Context, 1970–2020: Society, Religion, and Mission" (South Hamilton: Center for the Study of Global Christianity, 2013), 9.

11. Ed Stetzer, "Column: Christianity Isn't Dying," *USA Today*, October 18, 2010, http://www.usatoday.com/story/opinion/2012/10/18/christianity-christians-pew -research/1642315/.

12. Joshua Project, U.S. Center for World Mission, accessed August 15, 2014, http://joshuaproject.net/.

13. Darly Conner Blog. http://www.connerpartners.com/frameworks-and-processes /the-real-story-of-the-burning-platform, August 2012.

14. Kirsteen Kim and Andrew Anderson, eds., *Edinburgh 2010: Mission Today and Tomorrow* (Oxford: Regnum Books International, 2011), 194.

15. David Olson, *The American Church in Crisis: Groundbreaking Research Based on a National Database of Over 200,000 Churches* (Grand Rapids: Zondervan, 2008), 35ff.

16. Scott McConnell, "Research: Church Openings Outspace Closings," April 21, 2010, accessed July 29, 2014, http://www.lifeway.com/Article/LifeWay-Research-finds -church-openings-outpace-closings-but-support-for-church-plants-lacking.

17. Thom Rainer, "WANTED: More Outreach-Minded Churches," accessed July 29, 2013. http://www.churchleaders.com/outreach-missions/outreach-missions-articles/139407-wanted-more-evangelistic-churches.html.

18. Alvin L. Reid, *Radically Unchurched: Who They Are & How to Reach Them*, (Grand Rapids: Kregel Publications, 2002), 23.

19. "Status of Global Mission, 2014, in the Context of AD 1800–2025," accessed July 29, 2014, http://www.gordonconwell.edu/resources/documents/StatusOfGlobalMission.pdf.

20. Thom S. Ranier, *I Am a Church Member"* (Nashville: B&H Publishing Group, 2013), 5.

21. Daniel R. Sanchez, *Church Planting Movements in North America* (Fort Worth, TX: Church Starting Network, 2007), 18.

22. Christine Wicker, *The Fall of the Evangelical Nation: The Surprising Crisis Inside the Church*, (New York: HarperCollins, 2008), 93.

23. Ibid., ix.

24. Ronald J. Sider, "The Scandal of the Evangelical Conscience," accessed July 29, 2014, http://www.booksandculture.com/articles/2005/janfeb/3.8.html?start=4.

25. Lawrence K. Altman, "Study Finds That Teenage Virginity Pledges Are Rarely Kept," *New York Times*, March 10, 2004, accessed July 29, 2014, http://www.nytimes.com/2004/03/10/us/study-finds-that-teenage-virginity-pledges-are-rarely-kept.html.

26. Michael Horton, "Beyond Culture Wars," *Modern Reformation*, May–June 1993, 3.

27. Carole Fleck, "The Boomers Most Generous at Charitable Giving," *AARP Blog*, August 8, 2013, http://blog.aarp.org/2013/08/08/boomers-most-generous-at-charitable-giving.

28. John Dickerson, *The Great Evangelical Recession* (Grand Rapids: Baker Book, 2013), 71.

29. Emmanuel M. Katongole, "Christianity, Tribalism, and the Rwandan Genocide: A Catholic Reassessment of Christian 'Social Responsibility,'" quoted from *Logos: A Journal of Catholic Thought and and Culture 8, no. 3 (Summer 2005): 67–93*. Project Muse. http://muse.jhu.edu/journals/log/summary/v008/8.3katongole.html

30. Michael Gerson, "Michael Gerson: An America that is Losing Faith with Religion," *Washington Post*, March 25, 2013, accessed July 30, 2014, http://www.washingtonpost.com/r/2010-2019/WashingtonPost/2013/03/25/Editorial-Opinion/Graphics/Pew-Decline-of-Institutional-Religion.pdf Aggregated data from surveys conducted by the Pew Research Center for the People.

31. Brett Kunkle, "How Many Youth Are Leaving the Church?," February 24, 2009, accessed July 30, 2014, http://www.conversantlife.com/theology/how-many-youth-are-leaving-the-church.

32. C. Peter Wagner, *Church Planting for a Greater Harvest: A Comprehensive Guide* (Ventura: Regal Books, 1990), 11.

CHAPTER 2

1. Tony Miano and Matt Slick, "Is the Sinner's Prayer biblical or not?," Christian Apologetics and Research Ministry , accessed December 4, 2014, http://carm.org /sinners-prayer.

2. Leroy Eims, *The Lost Art of Disciple Making* (Grand Rapids: Zondervan, 2009) 16.

3. Dallas Willard, *The Great Omission: Reclaiming Jesus's Essential Teachings on Discipleship* (New York: HarperOne, 2006), v.

4. Alan Hirsch, *Disciplism: Reimaging Evangelism through the Lens of Discipleship* (ebook distributed by Exponential Resources, 2014), 17.

5. Scot McKnight, *King Jesus Gospel* (Grand Rapids: Zondervan, 2011), 28.

CHAPTER 3

1. George Hunter, *Church for the Unchurched*, (Nashville: Abingdon Press: 1996), 58.

2. Alan Hirsch, *The Forgotten Ways*, (Grand Rapids: Brazos Press; 2006), 25.

3. See chapter 6 for further explanation.

4. Chris Argyris, *Theory in Practice: Increasing Professional Effectiveness*. (San Francisco: Jossey-Bass, 1974).

5. David Watson, "Church Planting Essentials—Urban Church Planting," Touchpoint, *http://www.davidlwatson.org/2010/05/15/church-planting-essentials-urban-church-planting/*. David Watson was an International Mission Board nonresident missionary to the Bhojpuri people in India.

6. A Survey and Analysis of the Bhojpuri Church Planting Movement in Uttar Pradesh and Bihar, Northern India, October 2008 Executive Summary, 2.

7. Stephen Gray, *Planting Fast-Growing Churches* (St. Charles, IL: ChurchSmart Resources, 2007), 63.

8. Global Church Planting Network, "New Churches that May Be Needed," accessed August 15, 2014 http://www.gcpn.info/home/regions.

9. John L. Ronsvalle and Sylvia Ronsvalle, *The State of Church Giving through 2002,* 14th ed. (Champaign, IL: Empty Tomb, 2004), 36.

10. John S. Dickerson, *Great Evangelical Recession, The: 6 Factors That Will Crash the American Church . . . and How to Prepare,* Kindle ed. (Grand Rapids: Baker Publishing Group; 2013), 84.

    I concur with Dickerson, as long as we continue to pursue financially heavy strategies to fulfill the Great Commission we will fall further and further behind in our efforts to reach every people group.

11. Johnson et al, "Christianity in its Global Context," 8.

CHAPTER 4

1. Fox News Network. "Meet Joe Green, who walked away from a $10b Facebook fortune," accessed December 3, 2014, http://www.foxnews.com/tech/2012/01/31 /joe-green-walked-away-from-10b-facebook-fortune/.

2. Tim Hegg, "My Big Fat Greek Mindset, Part 1," (Tacoma, WA: TorahResource, 2006), 1, accessed August 15, 2014, www.torahresource.com/EnglishArticles/BigFat GreekMindsetPart1.pdf.

3. C. S. Lewis, *Mere Christianity* (UK: Geoffrey Bles, 1952; New York: HarperCollins, 2001), 38–39. http://merecslewis.blogspot.com/2010/11/atheism-turns-out-to-be-too -simple.html.

4. Roy Zuck, "Hebrew Words for 'Teach,'" *Bibliotheca Sacra* 121 (July-September 1964): 228–235 and "Greek Words for 'Teach,'" *Bibliotheca Sacra:* 122 (April–June 1965): 158–168.

5. J. P. Louw and E. A. Nida, *Greek-English Lexicon of the New Testament: Based on Semantic Domains* (New York: United Bible Societies, 1996).

CHAPTER 5

1. Parse, Ministry and Culture from Leadership Journal, "Willow Creek Repents?" *Christianity Today*, October 18, 2007, http://www.christianitytoday.com/parse/2007 /october/willow-creek-repents.html?start=2.

   He goes on to say, "What we should have done when people crossed the line of faith and become Christians, we should have started telling people and teaching people that they have to take responsibility to become "self feeders." We should have gotten people, taught people, how to read their Bible between service, how to do the spiritual practices much more aggressively on their own."

2. For more information see Contagiousdisciplemaking.org, as well as Accelerateteams .org.

3. Cityteam is a former rescue mission turned disciple-making organization. David Watson helped shape their thinking and connect them with movements around the world. www.cityteam.org/idisciple.

4. David Dunning and Justin Kruger, "Unskilled and Unaware of It: How Difficulties in Recognizing One's Own Incompetence Lead to Inflated Self-Assessments," *Journal of Personality and Social Psychology*, December 1999, Vol. 77, No. 6, 1121–1134.

CHAPTER 6

1. Benjamin Franklin, "The Price of Corn and Management of the Poor, 1776," Letter to the Public and Co., accessed August 15, 2014, *http://www.founding.com/founders library/pageid.2146/default.asp.*

CHAPTER 7

1. "Survey Shows How Christians Share Their Faith," Barna Group, January 31, 2005: "One of the key findings of the research was that a slight majority of born again adults - 55% - claimed to have shared their faith in Christ with a non-Christian during the prior 12 months. That figure has remained relatively constant during the past decade." *https://www.barna.org/barna-update/article/5-barna-update/186-survey-shows -how-christians-share-their-faith#.VFKD-RY8Ruk.*

2. Wisdom Quotes, accessed August 15,2014, *http://www.wisdomquotes.com/quote /epictetus-2.html.*

3. Dunning and Kruger, "Unskilled and Unaware of It: How Difficulties in Recognizing One's Own Incompetence Lead to Inflated Self-Assessments," 1121–1134.

4. Martin Luther, Defense and Explanation of All the Articles. Second Article (1521).

CHAPTER 9

1. C. S. Lewis, *Voyage of the Dawn Treader* (Pte. Limited, 1952; New York: HarperCollins Children's Books, 1994), 115–16.

2. Roland Allen, *Spontaneous Church Expansion of the Church* (Eugene, OR: Wipf & Stock Publishers, 1962), 40.

3. Daron Acemoglu and James A. Robinson, *Why Nations Fail* (New York: Crown, 2012), 429.

4. "Ignaz Semmelweis," accessed August 15, 2014, http://en.wikipedia.org/wiki/Ignaz _Semmelweis; "Semmelweis' Germ Theory" https://explorable.com/semmelweis -germ-theory.

5. Brian Eno, accessed August 15, 2014, http://en.wikipedia.org/wiki/Brian_Eno.

REFRACTION

GOD ALIGNS PEOPLE OF FAITH TO HIS PURPOSES

Thomas Nelson's Refraction collection of books offer biblical responses to the biggest issues of our time, topics that have been tabooed or ignored in the past. The books will give readers insights into these issues and what God says about them, and how to respond to others whose beliefs differ from ours in a transparent and respectful way. Refraction books cross theological boundaries in an open and honest way, through succinct and candid writing for a contemporary, millenial-minded reader.

LEARN MORE AT REFRACTIONBOOKS.COM

NOW AVAILABLE   NOW AVAILABLE   NOW AVAILABLE   NOW AVAILABLE   JULY 2015